C. G. Holmes

MARCH 1971

HOW TO GIVE A

FASHION SHOW

by

FRIEDA STEINMANN CURTIS

Book Division
Fairchild Publications, Inc.
New York

To my always helpful and understanding friend,
Phoebe Craig Hurty.

Table of Contents

TABLE OF CONTENTS

Introduction

Have you ever been called into the boss's office at the end of a hectic day to be greeted with, "Miss Gordon, I've been going over the figures of the ready-to-wear division today, and I've decided that what we need to pep them up is a fashion show. I'd like you to go to work on one immediately"?

Whether you are an old hand at fashion shows, or whether you never gave one in your life, you probably felt a cold shiver go down your back as you listened. From your own experience or from hearsay, there undoubtedly flashed through your mind visions of endless hours of work, of incredible moments of confusion, of unbelievable exhaustion. Yet you probably said quite calmly and meekly, "Yes, Mr. Jones, I'll get to work on it right away."

Not always, but all too often, decisions to give fashion shows are made as casually as that; and all too often the person who is given the responsibility for the show has to crowd it into an already full schedule. It is one thing to say, "Please do a fashion show," and quite another to bring that fashion show into being. There are almost literally thousands of details to attend to before the time comes for giving the signal to open the curtain. Yet, staggering as these details may appear at the beginning and snarled as the producer may become in them as the ensuing days go by, the show miraculously goes off with a flourish, if the entire project has been thought out clearly and if a logical plan has been followed. At the end, all the pieces fit into the pattern that has been painstakingly pre-determined.

The vital thing is to have a plan — a plan not only for a single show, but a blueprint for the entire business from the thinking stages to the final return of the merchandise to stock. Such a blueprint is insurance against discovering at the last minute —

often when it is too late to do anything about it — that one of the most important matters has been forgotten. It is like a recipe for baking a cake or like a set of plans for building a house; it gives assurance that things will turn out right at the end.

Fashion shows cost money. Fashion shows cause upheavals in the routines of almost any store. Fashion shows must produce results, or they represent losses to the store. Fashion shows are promotional devices, exactly like store displays or newspaper advertising or direct mail campaigns. They must be worked out as carefully and purposefully as are these other promotional efforts, if they are to bring returns comparable to the expenditure of money and energy they represent.

Many things must be weighed carefully and decided before it is time to say, "Let's give a fashion show." Much careful planning must be done before the fashion production is begun. To arrive at a working basis for the kind of fashion show that will make everyone, from the owner of the store to the porters, happy with it (and this is really a very large order), it is necessary to ask and to answer a number of leading questions, the first of which is:

Chapter 1

Why Give a Fashion Show?

The real reason why stores give fashion shows is *to sell merchandise.* There are people who will argue that fashion shows are presented primarily for the prestige value they have for a store; yet, unless the prestige a store acquires results in actual purchase by customers, it has no real value for the institution. A store endeavors to build its prestige in the community for the express purpose of developing confidence in the minds of those who buy so they will come into that store to buy goods.

When a store gives a fashion show in cooperation with a civic organization, it certainly gains prestige in that community; but unless it also gains in customers, it might better have given a check to some charity and let the matter of the fashion show go. When a store sends some of its fashion people into a neighboring town to give a program for the woman's club, it adds to its prestige in that town. Unless it also attracts some of those people into the store or enlarges its mail order business in that town, it has wasted its money and effort.

All fashion shows, it is true, do not result in immediate, measurable sales. This is especially true of those which introduce the fashions of the spring and fall seasons, as well as those given in cooperation with outside organizations. It may take several weeks, and sometimes even longer, to get the full benefits in sales of a fashion show. If, however, the business of the fashion departments shows steady, healthy growth, then fashion shows are undoubtedly an important factor in that advance.

Some fashion shows do show results in immediate, directly traceable activity in the departments which have participated in them. Such shows are generally ones which have been aimed at

1

a specific audience and have been given in such a way that the people attending have become closely identified with the narration and the models in the show. Shows presented for the mature woman, in which her figure problems are carefully analyzed, almost invariably create heavy activity in the women's shops immediately after the show. But whether the sales come right away or whether they are spread over a longer period, the basic reason for fashion presentations is *to sell merchandise.*

The desire to enhance the prestige of a store through a fashion show is a powerful, secondary motive for engaging in this sort of promotional effort. Like exciting window displays, like attractive counter displays, like beautiful store interiors — deep pile carpets, indirect lighting, luxurious divans, exquisite color schemes — parades of gorgeous, high-fashion costumes, done in exotic, richly perfumed settings, will stir audiences to a high pitch of enthusiasm and will produce in them a firm conviction that the store is an infallible fashion authority. Such shows identify the store with other fashion authorities, for when models seem to have stepped out of the pages of *Vogue* and *Harper's Bazaar,* the women viewing them become certain that the store can be trusted in its fashion judgment. Showing exclusive lines by the great American and foreign designers enhances the fashion position of the store, and as fashion-conscious customers talk about such shows, the reputation of the store spreads in ever-widening directions, resulting ultimately in that store's becoming known throughout the nation as a high-fashion institution.

Another reason why stores give fashion shows is that they have discovered the value of letting their customers see how they will look in the new fashions to be spotlighted in an approaching season. This is an important thing for stores to do at the beginning of any major season, especially if fashions are changing drastically. It was through clever use of fashion shows that many stores were able to sell the much-resisted "new look," after World War II. The majority of women are uncertain about the correctness of their fashion judgment; they don't know how clothes hanging on store racks will look on human forms; and they are most fearful about how those clothes will look on them. Women constantly appraise each other, not because they are always critical of each other, but because they are trying to see how they would look in the clothes the other women are wearing. So the wise fashion store will give its customers the opportunity to see how the new fashions look on live models. They will choose models, not too glamorous, who can wear different sorts of costumes selected to appeal to many tastes. Thus the customers can appraise the new styles in terms of themselves. Many a new idea in clothes has been sold to the public in this way, for when a woman finds herself thinking, "If that model can wear that dress, I can, too," another sale is three-fourths made. It won't be long until the spectator at the show finds herself in one of the store's dressing rooms decked out in a similar outfit.

Although the fact is not always recognized, every fashion show is, in a sense, an educational project. By selecting clothes that are most becoming to the models who show them; by adding to those clothes harmonious, smart, correct accessories, the store is teaching its patrons important lessons in the art of dressing. The store can go much further, however, in this mission of educating its public. Many women know very little about how to evaluate their own figure problems; they do not know when a garment is becoming and when it is not; they have never learned how to view themselves objectively. How eagerly these customers ask for advice and reassurance from the salespeople regarding their choices of clothing! How much more eagerly do groups of these customers respond to special fashion shows which teach their audiences how to study the human figure and how to select clothes that will give their wearers self-confidence and assurance!

The women who need basic fashion education are not confined to a single age group nor to any particular income bracket. With

3

only the simplest research and a lively imagination, they can be located easily, and they will attend the shows for them; furthermore, they will be grateful and enthusiastic. Many middle-aged women sorely need help in this direction. Business women of all ages are eager for special assistance in selecting wardrobes best suited to their lives and their budgets. Women of moderate means want to learn how to spend their money wisely to secure clothes in good taste. School teachers and professional women welcome shows concerned with their problems. Perhaps the greatest confirmation of women's desire for fundamental fashion education can be found in the enormous success of a number of well-known magazines devoted to this single undertaking. Shows appealing to special audiences like these can often be used to give new impetus to the business of ready-to-wear departments during off-seasons. Although it is generally true that the greatest amount of promotional effort should be expended when people are eager to buy, a well-dramatized show aimed at a particular group can stir those people to buy when they might not otherwise be interested in doing so.

There are quite a few possible answers to the question, "Why give a fashion show?" Never give a fashion show until this question has been answered satisfactorily. Never let anyone sell you the idea of giving a show "just because it would be nice to have one."

Chapter 2

Who Will Come to the Fashion Show?

This question means that the store must have a clear idea about what group, or what combination of its many varied patrons it wishes to attract by the show it intends to give. It is astonishing, when one takes time to analyze it, how many different kinds of people, how many different age groups turn to the same store for the satisfaction of their needs and desires. There are men and women — young, middle-aged, old; those with ample incomes, with moderate incomes, with low incomes. There are boys and girls — infants, young children, sub-teens, teen-agers — from homes in various income levels. Among these men and women and boys and girls are innumerable groupings based on the kind of work, the kinds of diversion, the kinds of lives they lead.

For a good many years, this analysis of stores' customers has been going on all over the country, and the results can be seen in all progressive stores in the ways in which merchandise is grouped for most effective selling. The budget shops, the better dress sections, the French rooms, the college and teen-age shops, the hat bars, the budget shoe departments, the entire downstairs store operations and numerous others have been developed, in order that customers may be served more efficiently and comfortably and so the store will sell more of its goods. As every good merchandiser knows, this classification of customers, this grouping of merchandise to appeal to different categories of customers has played a great role in the expansion and dollar increase of today's retail establishments.

5

Your Merchandise Reflects Your Customers

Just as the various units in the store tell the story of its varying customers, so does the merchandise. The stocks on the shelves and in the drawers reveal the fact that buyers are constantly busy analyzing their customers, trying to gauge what they will need, what they will like, what they will call for when they come to the store. What can the range of merchandise in the ready-to-wear and accessory divisions of the store tell the fashion coordinator about the store's clientele? Clothes and hats by top-flight designers, exquisite, expensive, handmade blouses, beautiful, high-priced gloves, handbags, scarfs and other accessories indicate that the store has wealthy, fashion-conscious customers. Here is a small but very important group for whom special fashion shows should be planned.

The greatest part of the stock in these two divisions (ready-to-wear and accessories) appeals to women belonging in the so-called "middle-income" sector of the population. In this group we find, according to the merchandise, a number of divisions: clothes bought for the older woman who requires half-sizes, clothes designed for the college girl, others for mothers-to-be, still others for the young teen-agers, clothes for those who prefer tailored classic styles and clothes for those who prefer softer, less severe lines. From these stocks, business women, teachers, young career girls, women doctors, lawyers, nurses select their wardrobes.

General and Special Audiences

When there is a seasonal fashion story to tell, all these groups can often be served by one comprehensive show — the show which presents high fashion and its moderately priced adaptations. All women want to see what the famous designers and the lesser ones, too, have to offer the American public. Even at the beginning of the fall and spring, however, it is sometimes much better to prepare a show or shows for groups of customers having the same interests, or the same incomes, or the same figure problems. Audiences are responding more and more to presentations directed particularly toward them, rather than merely including them in a broader, more diffused showing. While the older woman, for instance, may be concerned about the fashion forecasts of a new season, she may very well decide against going to a big revue of fashion, because her past experience has been that such revues rarely include clothes she can wear. "Yes," you'll hear one older woman say to another, as they walk out of your auditorium, "it was a nice show, but I can't wear any of those clothes." Certainly, no sales will result from their attendance. And perhaps the space they occupied would have been used by someone who was turned away, who would have bought as a result of seeing the performance.

That older woman, however, *can* be interested in a show and *will* buy, if the show has been arranged especially for her. There is an enormous potential for sound and profitable business among older women who, freed from the cares and expense of rearing families, are, often for the first time in their lives, able to satisfy their longings for becoming clothes. They have money to spend, but know little about how to spend it, and are eager for the fashion lessons a show can teach them.

Within the larger classification of business and professional women, there are several groupings worthy of separate fashion shows. The young career girl has many opportunities to see shows given particularly for her, and the most outstanding feature of these shows is the effort to keep the clothes shown within the budgets of these younger women. Among those business women not limited so severely in the matter of budget, there are equally excellent audiences. School teachers respond exceptionally well to shows given for them; other professional women — lawyers, doctors, business executives, directors and supervisors in the social agencies and in hospitals — want and urgently need help with their wardrobes. They will attend fashion shows designed for them, if they are properly approached. They will buy generously after such a show, if the proper arrangements are made to serve them quickly and efficiently.

7

Young mothers and mothers-to-be also like to attend shows dealing with their needs and with their income limitations. These shows can be used, too, to show children's clothes to best advantage. Another large and interesting audience can be found among the store's downstairs store patrons. These women rarely attend shows given in the upstairs auditorium or on the upstairs floors, but they will flock to a show presented in the downstairs store. Activity after such shows is proof of the wisdom of doing such fashion presentations.

What about the so-called "younger generation"? There are, of course, the college girls and teen-agers for whom shows have become a tradition in most stores. The teen-ager's younger sister, the "betwixt and betweener" or the sub-teen, until a few years ago the forgotten child of merchandising, is now being viewed as an important person in the fashion field. Manufacturers have been alerted by buyers to think of this group as distinct from the children's category, and many firms are designing clothes for this group that are increasing the potentials in junior merchandising. Fashion shows for both girls and boys in this age group have already proved profitable.

Mixed audiences, of men and women or high school boys and girls, present some fine fashion show possibilities. Such shows can produce spectacular results in sales, when they have been carefully thought out and produced, so that the male point of view, as well as the female, is catered to. What fascinates and intrigues a girl or woman may bore a man or boy to tears. It is possible, however, to give shows which will turn boredom into active interest and enthusiasm on the part of men and boys. When this is accomplished, the results are astonishing.

Fashion show audiences can also be classified according to the things they like to do in their leisure time. Ardent sportsmen and sportswomen, absorbed in varied sports — golf, tennis, riding, hunting, fishing, hiking, skiing, skating, sailing, swimming — are all extremely conscious of the clothes especially designed and appropriate for these active sports. Another natural audience grouping are the women who live in suburban areas

8

and who devote themselves to gardening, to semi-rural social affairs and small-town activities. An entire show can be done for dancing devotees, beginning with the colorful square-dancing costumes, then showing clothes for informal dances and finally glamorous evening wear.

Audiences can be grouped in many ways; it is the clever promotion-minded fashion coordinator who must see the potentials in her store's customers. She may, for instance, hit upon a wonderful idea, such as one fashion person did, of having a series of shows appealing to audiences in various "size" groups: one show for those who wear size 10, another for those wearing size 12, another for the 14's and one for the 16's. She may find an audience among the factory workers in her community, or she may do a show for the rural customers of her store.

The answers to "Who will come to our fashion show?" are many and depend upon all the other matters that must be dealt with. Until you know what sort of audience you will have, until you have decided which one of your many audiences your show is to attract, you cannot go on to answer the rest of the questions which must be answered before you are ready to give your show.

Chapter 3

What Kind of a Show Shall It Be?

From the most elaborate production to the simplest departmental floor-modeling, fashion shows fall into one of two general classifications: the fashion revue or parade, and the dramatized fashion show. The fashion parade, as the name implies, consists of a succession of models showing the clothes selected to tell the fashion story of the moment. It can be given on the selling floor with only a runway set up in an advantageous location. It can be presented in an auditorium with a simple background setting to suggest the season or merely with a plain backdrop. It can be held in a ballroom, a restaurant or any place where sufficient space is available for the models to show off the clothes to adequate advantage. Its only emphasis is on the clothes, and through them the show can be exciting and spectacular or merely commonplace. The dramatized fashion show, on the other hand, always has an idea or theme which gives unity to the entire production and which is expressed not only through the clothes but through the sequence in which they are shown, through changes of scenery, through the use of various properties and through the action — pantomime — of the models. The dramatized show creates an atmosphere or mood which enhances the clothes and induces the audience to feel as though they were part of the show. It is an atmosphere similar to that of the theatre, where, if the play is good, the spectators become a part of the performance.

Both kinds of shows offer a stimulating challenge to the

11

creative, imaginative fashion expert, provided she also has a sober awareness that somewhere in the background lurks the inexorable comptroller with his uncompromising questions about "How much is it going to cost?". It is hard, sometimes, for the fashion show producer to curb her wonderful flights of fancy, but this is where ingenuity has its day. Ingenuity brings profound satisfactions, too, especially when an effect can be fairly well achieved for half the original cost.

The Fashion Parade

The answer to the question, "What kind of a show shall it be?" depends upon two things: the over-all objectives of the show and the kind of audience you wish to attract. Stores have two big, important fashion seasons each year (spring and autumn) when fashion innovations and changes — expressed in new and often radically different designs; in daring, stimulating colors; in unusual fabrics; in countless accessories — are to be shown to all its customers. At these seasons, the fashion parade is often the best way in which to tell the comprehensive fashion story. What's new? What's different? What's the fashion future? These are the questions all the store's customers want to see answered. As the models parade down the runway, each one looking as though she had just stepped out of the pages of the nation's finest fashion magazines, the merchandise unfolds the tale of the new, the exciting, the provocative in clothing for the coming season. The clothes are the entire show, and nothing should be spared in making each costume the acme of perfection. This is the time when all age groups and every sector of the buying public can be appealed to, those in the top income brackets as well as those in the more modest ones. The fashion story is being told for everyone.

The fashion parade is also a favorite when the store provides a show for the benefit of some charity which an organization in the community sponsors. The fashion show may be the feature attraction at a luncheon, tea, cocktail party or ball; and again, the clothes are the show. These are the times when the store can show its most luxurious furs, its most glamorous costumes, exquisite hostess gowns, most daring and striking accessories. Sometimes, when such affairs include both men and women in the audience, special attractions should be included. A movie actress and a famous actor, beautiful models from New York, and a clever master of ceremonies give added interest. Most careful attention must be expended on the lighting for such a show, and there must be excellent music to make every new entrance exciting and to keep the show moving.

Sometimes the store wants to show its high-fashion customers its designer collections in gowns, ensembles and millinery. These invitational collections — teas or cocktail parties — embody all the elegance of entertaining in a home or a club. Every detail must be planned meticulously, from beautiful decorations and delicious refreshments faultlessly served, to the costumes to be shown. This is an intimate fashion parade, but the emphasis is on the clothes, the designers, the fashion prestige of the store-host. Models may walk among the tables, while the guests are being served. More effective as to presentation and sales results, however, is to wait until the serving is finished. Then the fashion commentator tells the story of each costume as it appears, emphasizing the store's fashion leadership, the famous couturiers it features, and its constant concern for its most discriminating clientele.

A small, select showing can be held in a secluded salon, when the collection of one designer is to be presented. On such occasions, the designer is generally present to speak informally about his clothes. The store's fashion coordinator generally assists with accessorizing the costumes and seeing to it that each model is turned out to perfection. Nothing more than the beauty of the salon and fashions is needed to make such a showing a success.

The fashion parade, large or small, requires as much perfection as possible in each outfit; the best lighting available; sprightly, lively music, but not too loud; good interesting commentary, never wordy; an even, smooth, never-lagging pace.

13

The Dramatized Story

When the answer to the question, "What kind of a show shall it be?" is "Let's give a dramatized show," additional factors become important. The dramatized show tries to make the spectators idenitfy themselves with the models. Such a show endeavors, in a limited way to be sure, to do what every play on the stage or screen tries to do — make the audience members of the cast. When the spectators hate the villain and love the hero and heroine in a play, they have become part of the play. So when the action on the stage and runway causes the onlookers to think of themselves as part of the show and makes them feel as though they are wearing the clothes being shown, they have become part of the show. After such identification, the chances for many sales of fashion show merchandise are excellent.

This sort of show demands accurate knowledge of the daily lives and concerns of the people for whom it is being planned. This is where sympathetic imagination can go to work. The fashion coodinator must put herself into the very shoes of her prospective audience to get ideas for her show that will be familiar and will give the show an atmosphere of reality. She must ask herself such questions as: What do these people do for a living and how much do they earn? How old are they? What do they do in their leisure time? And any others that will help to shed light upon her audience.

The Older Woman's Show

One special group for whom the dramatized show is ideal is composed of older women, not too old, who have spent little time on their appearance during the early years, but who have fulfilled their family duties and at last are free to consider themselves. The older woman has money to spend, but often doesn't know how to spend it. She is thirsty for knowledge about selecting becoming clothes and about what to do for her figure problems. She is probably in her late forties or early fifties. "There's some life in the old girl yet," you'll hear her say, half in jest and definitely half in earnest. She isn't ready to be put on the shelf. She wants to go places and do things; she wants to have some fun, now that her children are grown. She has become convinced by all the shouting headlines in magazines, car ads, radio and television commercials that "you, too, can look years younger!!" But how? How? How?

This is where the store can step into the picture. A single show for such an audience, properly promoted, will prove how much such endeavors are appreciated. This show must start, of course, with figure problems. Scene I will be, for instance, a woman's boudoir, a fitting background for discussing the intimate details of figure-control and also for showing how well-constructed foundation garments are the first requirement in the process of acquiring a new appearance. Such a scene should include a discussion of diets and exercising which can change flabby, sagging muscles into firm flesh. This scene can be used to show the store's seldom-appreciated wealth of lingerie. There is an important story to tell about slips that fit to perfection; about nightgowns and pajamas that provide comfort and glamor; about robes that are serviceable and festive. With skillful comments, the women of the audience will become a part of the scene without realizing what is happening. After the show, they will flock to the corset and lingerie departments.

Scene II takes up the next vital matter for the woman seeking to make herself over —coiffures and make-up. This can be a kind of interlude, played out in front of the curtain, or again with a bedroom setting. A few models, having varying facial characteristics, will have their hair combed while the commentator discusses the means which the hair stylist has used to create the most becoming coiffure for that particular model. The cutting and shaping, the permanent, the shampooing and setting will already have been done, but when the model has been combed and is ready for the runway, the audience will know exactly how the final effect was secured. The make-up process can be done similarly and combined with the coiffure for each model. A quick transformation from no make-up to swiftly-applied and highly becoming make-up is one of the most dramatic tricks that can be used in such a scene.

Scene III can present the woman at home. It will begin with a showing of attractive house or daytime dresses and aprons; then follow simple, well-designed afternoon dresses, some for ordinary home wear, others to be worn for at-home entertaining. The scene ends with a group of charming hostess gowns.

Scene IV can deal with the woman shopper or traveler. This part of the show presents suits, coats and ensembles of all kinds. It also highlights the accessories that can dress basic clothes up or down. The scene can be a store fitting room with a background of mirrors, at least a large triple mirror and more, if it is at all possible, so that the audience can watch the fitting of the models from numerous angles. Figure problems are again the topic, and the commentator will have much to say about suitable styles in suits, coats and dresses for mature figures. She will discuss correct sleeves and necklines, selection of fabrics and colors, and the models will exemplify the points being made. This scene will also be concerned with the proper hats for different facial and figure types. Each model, as she appears, can take a seat before the mirror and be shown several hats by the salesperson in the show. Some of the hats can be completely wrong for the model, and the inappropriateness of these hats will be pointed out. At last, the exactly correct, smartest and most becoming hat will be chosen, and the model can proceed down the runway. This same process of explanation, with an occasional trial and error interlude can be applied to all accessories.

Scene V will prove that older women no longer need suppress their yearnings for glamor clothes. Here can be shown smart cocktail suits and dresses, intriguing separates, elegant dinner gowns and sophisticated decollete. Furs, jewelry, beautiful footwear, stunning evening wraps can be used to heighten the effect of this last scene and bring the show to an exciting conclusion.

To send the audience into enthusiastic applause at the end of such a show, and more important, to send them to the ready-to-wear departments in eager search of new wardrobes, requires a number of skills in addition to that of being able to select clothes for the show. Obviously, the first is the ability to tell the story of the show effectively. Probably the next most important thing is to have models who are not too different from the people who attend the performance. This is a point which is often overlooked; for the show directed toward the older woman, it can spell the difference between spectacular success and dismal failure. If any woman is heard to remark as she leaves the hall, "Well, those young, beautiful models can wear *anything*. But just let *me* try to wear those clothes!" then the show has been a failure, though it went off without a mishap. The kind of remark that indicates success might go like this: "You know, Sarah, I believe *I* could wear that blue dress in the third scene," and "Im sure that dinner dress — you know, the rust satin one — would be just the right thing for me to wear to the dinner dance we're going to next month." Such talk means that the women have become identified with the action and clothes in your show. Sales, often unbelievably large ones, come from such identification.

Variations of the Older Woman's Show

We're all familiar with the musical term, "variations on a theme." Just as composers can create many variations on the same musical theme, so can fashion experts conceive variations on the same fashion show theme. For instance, the show for the older woman could be made into an effective "right and wrong" presentation with every point brought out dramatically by having one model dressed incorrectly and another turned out faultlessly. For such a show, you have to use pairs of models having approximately the same type of figure, one pair of short heavy women, one pair of tall, heavy-busted women, another pair of average proportions, and another of heavy-hipped women. Each pair could alternate the right and wrong clothes, so that the lesson being taught — that it is the correct selection of clothes which makes the difference — would be made that much more emphatic.

It is also possible to expand the ideas outlined in the five scenes of the older woman's show into a series of performances, each one devoted to one phase of the over-all grooming problem; that is, one session devoted to figure-control; one to hair, cosmetics and the selection of becoming hats; one to choosing suitable suits, coats and dresses with the appropriate accessories; and one for correct at-home wear. Women will pay for the privilege of attending such a series, and often a sizeable amount of the expense involved can be recovered through these admissions. When a fee is charged, it is good to present each woman attending with a multigraphed or printed brochure which covers the basic information given during each session. Manufacturers are sometimes willing to share the expense of preparing such material, for the privilege of being listed at the end of the booklet as having participated in the project. This provides another means by which brand name merchandise or *the* manufacturer can be promoted. Cosmetic firms will often cooperate generously, by giving samples of make-up or invitations to customers to have complimentary make-ups. The store's beauty salon can take part in the promotion by giving the holder of a lucky ticket a complete hair re-styling. The resultant newspaper publicity, which an alert store can secure from such a fashion-education undertaking, will more than compensate for the time and money invested.

Another variation of this same theme was done by *Good Housekeeping Magazine* years ago. Those who were working in the fashion business in the 1930's will never forget the experiment this publication's fashion department made with a Westchester housewife, who had arrived, as she put it, at the "dubious age." To prove that knowledge about clothes selection and careful attention to the principles of line and color can transform the dowdy, middle-aged woman into a well-dressed, attractive-looking person, Mrs. Agnes Smedley, the housewife, became the guinea pig for this experiment. There followed untold numbers of consultations, of fittings, of revampings of one sort or another, until one fine day there emerged from the brown cocoon that had been Mrs. Smedley, a rejuvenated, recreated woman who bore only a fleeting resemblance to her old self. Mrs. Smedley had been taught how to dress and groom herself correctly from the foundation garment up and out. A more profound change had also taken place, for all the latent sense of humor, all the submerged sparkle of an earlier Mrs. Smedley had been released during the revamping process. She had been transformed in appearance (and without the loss of a single pound); she had been transformed psychologically. She, as an individual, had a future.

The story of this experiment, when it appeared in the February, 1939 issue, caused a stir in the *Good Housekeeping* world. When Mrs. Smedley began her personal tour of the country to show and tell women that this was not an editor's dream but a living actuality, there was real excitement. Alert department stores were delighted to share in this excitement and profit from it, too. Combining a fashion show of their merchandise for the mature woman with Mrs. Smedley's appearance, they used the project to the fullest advantage.

If any fashion or promotion person needed confirmation that here was a performance that really interested and involved the audience, she had only to watch the intent faces of the women who were present to be completely convinced. The show started with Mrs. Smedley's appearance on the stage in a brown tweed suit, somewhat wrinkled, but of good sturdy material, exactly the kind of suit a matron could wear until it dropped off her; "it was *so* practical!" Mrs. Smedley, late fortyish, fitted snugly into the suit, and the broad expanse of her hips had that comfortable air and that baggy look with which everyone is familiar. Her brown hat was suitably "tailored looking," the kind of hat you could slam on your head as you rushed out the door to catch the 9:50 for a day's shopping in town for the children and the house. A severe shirtwaist (unadorned), worn (but good) brown leather bag, oxfords and gloves completed her outfit. She was clothed, Mrs. Smedley explained, according to her mother's precepts of years ago, as a sensible, conservative wife and mother should be clothed. She had stuck to that formula for "Heavens knows how long!" As a matter of fact, Mrs. Smedley could not remember when the mainstay of her wardrobe had not been this or a similar suit which had served her for all occasions except those when she wore a housedress or when she occasionally dressed up in an afternoon dress. No, she went on to say, it wasn't because she couldn't afford clothes; she couldn't afford the time it took to select them, she had such difficulty making up her mind. All that had changed, however, from the moment she had placed her person at the disposal of the fashion editor of *Good Housekeeping*. Since then, her eyes had been opened, and she'd learned, not only how to select her clothes, but also, most of all, what fun and resulting pleasure for others could be derived from it. With other and amusing comments, the star of the show discussed the figure problems of mature women and explained how they could learn to minimize their defects and enhance their assets by correct selection of garments. The real proof of her statements came when she reappeared on the stage after a brief disappearance, transformed from the nondescript woman she had been at first into a smart, well-groomed, assured person. She had discarded the old girdle she'd been wearing (she held it up for a good laugh), and had donned a sleek foundation garment which formed the basis for her new appearance. The suit she wore was of soft, lightweight wool, and its lines were correct for Mrs. Smedley's figure. The upper-arm and hip-line bulges had vanished; there was continuity and grace in the ensemble. So the show went on, from one type of outfit to another, each supplemented by costumes from the store's own stocks, and each dramatically telling the story all the audience wanted to hear — that women *can* look well in their clothes; they don't have to settle into the slough of fashion despondency at middle-age; that "life *can* begin at forty."

High School Fashion Shows

The dramatized fashion show is excellent for audiences of middle-aged women, but its appeal is not limited to this one group. If ever the dramatic show pays dividends, it does so in high school fashion shows. Some of the sensational success of

20

teen-age merchandising can be traced to the fashion shows which have tied in with adolescent preoccupations and have so involved the students in the show's action that their enthusiasms for the clothes in the show have been aroused. The trick with the teen-age show has been to devise scenes and action that are authentic and to use students as models.

One of the most successful teen-age fashion shows ever given was one in which both boys and girls were models. It was difficult, of course, to get high school boys to be fashion show models, but some skillful use of psychology resulted in securing a few popular athletes from two high schools of the city. It was not long, thereafter, until all the high schools had enlisted a satisfactory number of acceptable boy models. The boys were then paired off with an equal number of attractive girls, also from the various schools. All the modeling for the entire show was done in pairs, thus affording opportunity for showing all kinds of boys' clothing as well as girls' clothing. The effectiveness of this single device was enormous, for each girl was a-flutter over modeling with an important boy of the high school, and each boy was flattered by the attention bestowed upon him by a pretty girl. This pairing of the boys and girls also became known in the high schools, and excited conversation about it filled the corridors, building up to fever-pitch as the day for the show approached. *Everyone* was determined to go to that show.

Meanwhile, problems of dramatizing the show effectively had to be solved. A plan was made, and the student-models were asked for suggestions to make the scenes and action as life-like as possible. It was like doing a school play. When the curtain finally went up on the day of the show, the first scene revealed an after-school hang-out, with tables and chairs, a Coke-bar, and the inevitable "juke box" playing a hit of the moment. The audience, jammed as tightly as possible into the auditorium, broke into thunderous applause, as they recognized their fellow-students, some sitting at the tables, some leaning over the Coke-bar, one or two at the "juke box." Then pair after pair, attired in the latest school-time fashions, strolled down the runway and back to the stage to the "juke box" music. The commentator, a young radio celebrity at the moment the idol of the adolescents, had been coached in what he was to say about the merchandise, but had been allowed free rein with his "ad-libbing." Every couple got a hand; every person in the audience got the fashion message.

The next scene showed the box office of a movie house; it was "date night." Two by two the couples appeared at the window for their tickets, this time modeling suits, coats, rain-wear and so on. Then followed a living room scene where an informal party was going on, offering the setting and action for showing dressier clothes of great variety. Last of all, came a softly lit terrace scene, where couples in evening clothes were dancing. Glamorous girls in formal wear and boys in tuxedos or in white trousers and dark blue coats made unforgettable pictures as they came down the runway.

And what of the response in cold hard cash to such a show? It was unprecedented! It resulted in mounting sales in the girls' departments, of course, but it was in the boys' section where the returns were most remarkable. Never before had the store done such business in boys' outfits—school wear and especially formal wear. Almost all the models bought some of the clothes they had shown, and their friends and acquaintances followed suit.

The Camping Show

Another dramatized show which can increase the business of all boys' and girls' departments, beginning at the five-year level and including high school students, is a camping show. Stores that have Girl Scout, Boy Scout or Campfire concessions can highlight all the official uniforms and equipment available to members of these groups. Even more important, however, are the many functional and attractive play clothes which mothers and their campers are anxious to see. Settings and action for such a show offer many possibilities. One show might start, for instance, with a railroad platform or a bus station background. Here the eager campers are dressed for travel and are carrying the latest in strong, durable camp luggage. In this scene summer outfits for the mothers, who are seeing their children off, can also be shown. The next scene might be a camp bunk house, or a playground for the showing of active play clothes for various age groups. Then would come a swimming-pool scene to show children's and adults' swimsuits and accessories. Finally, there could be a scene in the camp recreation hall as the campers assemble for some special program. Outdoor clothes, sweaters, skirts and other warm things for chilly weather at camp would be modeled. To add liveliness to this scene, some of the children might do a square dance or perform one of the ceremonies of camp life. A number of variations on the camping theme, depending upon the locality of the store and the preferences of its customers, could be worked out. Such a show is certain to boost the sales in camp equipment and raise the store's prestige as camping headquarters in that community.

The Sports Show

The store that is eager to build its sportswear and equipment business can give a sports fashion show, appealing to both men and women. Such a show, using both sexes as models, can increase sales of golf, tennis, riding and other sports clothes, as well as the equipment used to participate in these sports, such as golf clubs, tennis rackets, outdoor equipment — barbecue sets, outdoor furniture, picnic baskets, and other items. One scene could show riding clothes, ranging from the most formal attire to Western outfits suitable for dude-ranch wear. Another scene could highlight golf, tennis, and other such active sports clothes for both men and women. Swimming and beach costumes, sailing and yachting attire could come next. Hunting clothes, skiing and skating ensembles would have important places in some areas. The final scene might be around a campfire for the presentation of comfortable relaxation clothes. Here the out-door cooks, dressed in all the new regalia, would reign supreme.

The Career Girl Show

The career girl has already received much attention from stores, but this market and the one that can be developed among older business women, should never be neglected. Here, too, the dramatized show can be used to good advantage. In preparation for the career girl show, it is sometimes wise to consult with personnel directors of the leading businesses of the city, asking them what ideas about office grooming and behavior they would like to have emphasized in the show. Such consultation will gain prestige for the store and will enlist the help of businesses in publicizing the show. If career girls are to be used as models, the personnel directors will find the best people in their organizations for the job. The models will give valuable suggestions for making the show more real and thus more successful. The first scene could be in a personnel office, presenting clothes suitable for job interviews, as well as clothes for office wear. Suits, coats, basic dresses would be shown. Next, could be the office at the end of the day, when the models would show changes of accessories from daytime to after-work things. The many versatile clothes could thus be given full attention. Another scene could show the business girl at home and would include relaxation clothes and home-entertaining ensembles. Last, of course, would come the glamor clothes.

The Bridal Show

The bridal show is, perhaps, one of the easiest and most delightful to dramatize. Scenes can be arranged to start with a trousseau shopping tour; an afternoon shower for the bride; a trousseau tea; and finally the wedding. Not all bridal shows must end with the wedding, however; a most dramatic method is to start the show with the altar tableau and the march down the aisle. Then can follow the wedding reception, presenting correct attire for youthful, middle-aged and older guests. A boudoir interlude, with the bride changing from her bridal gown to her travel clothes and showing the bridal lingerie

24

could come next; and finally, the going-away clothes complete with luggage. Another bridal show is one which is divided into three sections, each devoted to showing a trousseau which can be purchased for a certain amount of money. Each scene would therefore include lingerie, travel clothes, play clothes for the bridal trip and the wedding gown. This kind of show is especially appropriate in times when people must spend their money to greatest advantage. It is necessary to select merchandise for the budget bridal show very carefully, so that contrasts in price will not be too great.

Knowledge of the production techniques of both the fashion parade and the dramatized show enables a store to plan a fashion show program providing interest, excitement and variety for its customers.

Chapter 4

Who Will Be the Models?

Although stores find that it is advantageous to use amateur models for certain kinds of shows from time to time, the first duty of the fashion coordinator in this regard is to develop a nucleus of trained, reliable models who are easily available and who know how to proceed with the job in a thoroughly business-like manner.

How does one go about finding the kinds of models the store needs? One good source of models is the sales force and the friends of salespeople. Another is the applicants who seek such jobs; still another is from among the amateurs who appear in a single show; and last, models can sometimes be secured through newspaper advertising. Occasionally, a model with experience will be available, but mostly the models must be trained by the fashion department.

Some stores have found it profitable to model clothes on the ready-to-wear floors and in their tearooms. This practice makes it possible for the fashion coordinator to try out promising salespeople who may eventually become the permanent models for the store, in addition to doing a certain amount of selling. Such a group of models who are always available, and who have constant practice in showing clothes, are invaluable to the fashion department. They know the stock; they know how to accessorize costumes; they know how to follow directions; they know how to appear on the runway. They can also assist with fittings for large shows and ones in which amateurs are used. When the store has such a group, every effort should be made to include in it some with figures which at least approximate those of the customers who will see them in shows or modeling on the floor. Of course, every woman would like to be tall and slender, but statistics make it clear, as does gazing at crowds of shoppers, that the majority of women are not Venus de Milos. One of the store's models, therefore, should be a well-built, statuesque woman, not too heavy but certainly not thin, who can wear a size 16 or 18 and make a very smart appearance. It is also a good idea to have a white or grey-haired woman, with a young face and a medium-sized figure, as a permanent model. Add to these, two younger girls, size 10 and 12, and you will have a fine group around which you can always build a satisfactory show.

Four models, however, are not enough for a regular show (eight is the minimum), so it is vital to build up a reserve of models who can be trained, little by little, to do the work in a professional manner and who are willing to work only when the store needs them. The store's sales force can again be tapped for such occasional models, but there is a difficulty in having too many salespeople on the reserve list. Often the times when they are needed for fashion shows are also the busiest times in their departments, and it is hard for the buyer to do without them. These people are best kept for the inevitable, last-minute emergencies — the times when a model suddenly comes down with the flu or the mumps.

Salespeople can be excellent talent scouts for the fashion department, however, if their services are properly enlisted. From among their friends, good models can often be found; and sometimes customers, whom salespeople know well, can be recruited as models. When stores give shows for organizations which furnish the models, the fashion coordinator has new contacts for possible models. The search for good material can never stop; the fashion coordinator must have the patience to interview many people who will not do for the sake of finding a few who will be exactly right. Gradually, she can build a file of names of suitable, reliable, efficient models. Under each name, she should list the model's measurements, her hair and complexion shades, her age, and the shows in which she has appeared. When the need arises, all that will then be necessary *is* to call in those models who will best serve the purposes of the projected show.

Qualifications for Models

What are the qualifications of a good model? First of all, regardless of her size, her body should be well-proportioned; it is important that she be able to wear the clothes she will be asked to model without alterations since alterations are not only expensive, but they also make it impossible to sell the clothes after they have been modeled. The next requirement is a good, clear complexion and nice skin. The hair must be well cared-for and relatively easy to manage. The posture and walk must be fairly good, although models can be trained to hold themselves better and to walk more satisfactorily. Real beauty is rare, but a pleasant, friendly expression can be required of all models. The models must have a certain amount of self-confidence, for lack of it will result in self-consciousness and consequent inability to show the clothes to best advantage. Above all, the prospective model must look upon modeling as strictly a business proposition. She must realize that personal feelings must be controlled, and really have no place in business. She must be willing to do whatever is asked of her, and to work at all times for the best effects for the show.

How to Train Models

How does the fashion coordinator train models who have good potentials but who lack some of the knowledge and experience necessary in a first rate performance? Walking with grace and ease is the first thing to be developed. It can be taught by presenting a few simple rules for posture and walking and through consistent, supervised practice of those rules. To avoid improper strain in the body, models should be made to realize that good posture and walking depend upon being able to control the movements of the body without any stiffening or tightening of the muscles. Controlled relaxation is the goal toward which they must strive. To achieve this controlled relaxation, the chest must be lifted, the weight must be lifted from the waist, but the shoulders must be allowed to rest naturally without tension. The model should imagine at all times that she is bringing the backbone and the abdomen together, although she will never actually do so. This idea of bringing the backbone or spine and the abdomen together, prevents, without strain, the sagging of the stomach muscles or the protrusion of the hips.

With the body in the alignment brought about by lifting the waist and chest muscles and bringing the spine and abdomen together, it now becomes possible to walk with assurance and grace. Here, the most important single idea is to make the movement of the legs originate at the hips, not at the knees. Swinging the legs from the hips, forward and backward, is a good preparation for practicing walking, for this emphasizes the fact that the impetus for walking must come from the hips but it also keeps the knees from stiffening or bending too much. As the model walks down the runway, she should place her feet on two lines about two inches apart, which may have been drawn on the runway for practice purposes. These lines should never be used to the point where the model feels a sense of strain in stepping on them, for then the aim of achieving *controlled relaxation* is defeated. Some instructors in walking say that the knees should touch each other lightly as one walks, for this assures the legs being sufficiently close together to make a graceful appearance at all times. Some experts believe it wise to teach models to toe out a tiny bit in order to assure accurate body-balance. The effect to be worked for at all times is a simple, easy forward motion of the body, without shoulder or hip-swinging, and without the awkwardness of placing the feet too far outward or too far inward. When such a walk has become habitual, the arms and hands will hang easily and naturally at the sides and will swing just enough to suit the motion of the body; the head will be held up in a relaxed and assured position, not be pushed forward nor allowed to droop.

It is a good idea to rate models, from time to time, on their posture, grace, facial expressions and figures. This can be made into an interesting group project by having all the models rate each other after a preliminary discussion of the principles involved in good modeling. A rating sheet, such as the one on the next page, can be used for this purpose.

Working with the Models

In working with the models, the fashion coordinator has many obligations. She must have the same objective attitude toward the models which she demands of them. There is no room for displays of temperament on the part of the director or the participants in the show. Any indications the director sees of the model's feeling that *she* is on parade, instead of the clothes being on parade, should be dealt with as soon as possible by taking the model inconspicuously aside and explaining things to her. The director should *never* embarrass nor humiliate a model, no matter what the provocation, for such treatment never accomplishes the desired results and only creates bad feeling among all the models. The fashion coordinator should work constantly to create a feeling of teamwork among the models, by making them all feel that they have much to contribute, that upon them rests the ultimate success or failure of the show. Good, harmonious relations with the models will smooth many a rough spot in a show and will assure an excellent performance.

The Use of Amateur Models

When should the store use amateur models? To answer this question, one must be able to weigh the advantages and disadvantages carefully and then come to the best possible conclusion. The disadvantages in using amateurs are many: First, amateurs rarely have the poise, the knowledge of how to walk on a runway, the self-confidence necessary to show clothes well. They know nothing about the behind-the-scenes discipline which must be maintained, if the show is to go off correctly. They have decided opinions about what they want to wear and what they don't want to wear, and often these opinions clash with the objectives of the show. They are not prompt for

RATING SHEET FOR MODELS

Date..

Give one (1) to ten (10) points for each. The highest possible score is 40. In judging grace, look for ease in movement of hands, arms, feet.

Name	Posture	Grace	Facial Expression	Figure	Total

rehearsals, and they expect special privileges, because they are sometimes "donating" their services.

The advantages in using amateurs, however, sometimes overbalance the disadvantages. When the store is trying to gain acceptance among certain groups in the community, and it agrees to provide a show for some worthy cause, it is a good idea to let the organization provide the models. Nothing is so revealing to outsiders as to work closely with a store's executives on a project of this kind. They learn something of the store's point of view, and become sympathetic to some of its problems. Later, they are proud to talk about the experience, and that conversation arouses others' interest in the store. Much the same thing occurs when young business girls model in a career girls' show. The store becomes home to them, in a sense, and they turn to it for further help with their clothing problems.

The high school students who model in teen-age shows are amateurs, but they are usually paid for their services. Paying them makes it possible for the director of the show to require certain things which she could hardly expect from unpaid amateurs. She can require paid amateurs to be on time at rehearsals, to do exactly what they are told to do; thus some of the disadvantages are overcome. There is still much extra coaching to be done, however, with those who are untrained, but the store which gives teen-age shows often will soon have a number of students who can be considered almost professional.

Probably the greatest benefit to be gained from using amateurs in fashion shows is the fact that the audience come to see their friends, and a general feeling of goodwill toward the store is produced. The models and their friends often make purchases they might not have made, and they initiate the habit of shopping in the store.

Chapter 5

What Merchandise Shall Be Shown?

When you've decided upon the kind of show you are going to give and who your models will be, do you go to the ready-to-wear departments and start fittings for the show? No, you certainly do not, if you want to be sure your show accomplishes its objectives. It takes just as much planning and analysis to decide what merchandise you will show as it does to decide for whom you will give the show.

Dealing with the Buyer

It is at this point that the wise fashion coordinator turns to the buyers for suggestions and help. It is true that buyers sometimes are not very enthusiastic about fashion shows, and why should they be? To many buyers, fashion shows are merely terrible disrupters of their departments. Although they know their stocks better than anyone else does, they are never consulted about the clothes to be presented in the show. No one has ever explained to them how the fashion show promotes the ready-to-wear sections of the store; no one has ever convinced them that the basic purpose of the show is to sell their stocks. They have simply been expected to clear the decks and throw open their stocks when the fashion people descend upon their departments. They have been plagued with swarms of models running around their sections, making remarks about the inadequacy of the stock and snatching things from the racks practically from under the customers' fingers. The smart and truly successful fashion director understands the buyer's side

from beginning to end. She trains her staff to give all consideration to the buyer during an admittedly trying time for everyone.
She asks for the buyer's opinions and help, instead of disregard-
ing and antagonizing her. When buyers are thus included in
the selection of the merchandise, they not only give valuable
assistance, but they also become interested and enthusiastic
about the show.

Merchandise for the Seasonal Show

The kinds of merchandise to be shown will depend on the
type of show and the audience toward whom it is being directed.
When the show is the seasonal presentation, then the best
examples of the season's fashion trends are culled from every
ready-to-wear department — the Gown Room, Better Dresses,
Budget Shop, Suit and Coat Shop, Sports Shop, College Shop
and so on. All accessory departments — millinery, hat bar, gloves,
handbags, hosiery, jewelry, scarfs — are also scanned. Each buyer
will have things she has chosen most carefully for their fashion-
rightness and excellent values. Together, these many items will
encompass the entire range of fashion and price; they will
present a comprehensive story that will appeal to all the
store's customers.

The seasonal show must impress upon its audience the fact
that the store has all the diversified designs, all the newest
fabrics, all the most desired colors, in various price lines. In
selecting the suits for such a show, for instance, the fashion
coordinator should include at least one of every style in fashion
— the bolero suit, the dressmaker suit, the very sporty suit, and
conservative tailored suit, the long jacket and the short jacket
suit. The same breadth of choice should be used in determining
the dresses, coats, sports costumes to be included. So, also, must
the fabric picture be presented, by including examples of whatever weaves and textures are favorites of the times. Last, but by
no means least, color should be highlighted, with variations and
successions of the newest shades being used to achieve the
most striking effects of the show.

When a complete survey of available merchandise has been made, each outfit chosen must be assigned to the model best suited to show it. Sometimes, the only way to be certain of obtaining the best effect is by the old trial and error method. This takes time and is very wearing, but the conscientious fashion person will make no compromises here. She will be absolutely certain that each model is wearing exactly the correct and most becoming things. She will also keep constantly before her the necessity for selecting clothes and accessories that are in the same price brackets. Because she takes her job seriously and because she wants the store to reap the maximum benefits from the show, she will stick with the task of selection, until she is completely satisfied in every detail.

Merchandise for the Dramatized Show

Selecting the clothes for a dramatized show requires great care, for every piece must convey with clarity and force the intended message. When the show is for career girls, for example, price and style are of primary concern. Every piece must be within the budget limits of the audience, but there must be variety and fashion as well. It is the fashion coordinator's business to convince her audience through the clothes she shows that her store cannot be surpassed in style and price. Just as the clothes being shown in the career girls' show must conform to their budgets, so must the accessories be moderately priced. It is very tempting to a fashion expert to combine an extravagant hat and handbag with a modestly priced dress, when the ensemble can thereby be made more striking and beautiful. If the customer is always kept in mind, however, it will appear ridiculous to suggest that she pay twice as much for her hat as she does for her dress. Women of moderate incomes do break over the traces, once in a while, and buy something foolishly expensive, but they go to fashion shows to learn how to avoid such folly. If the effect of an outfit is achieved by using accessories out of proportion in cost to the basic costume, a customer may say to herself, "The only way that dress would look like anything is if you put an expensive hat with it, and I can't afford such hats." Lost — another sale. Most accessory departments have been built on the idea of having many moderately priced sets of accessories to provide interesting and stimulating variety to a modest basic wardrobe.

Merchandise for a "Right and Wrong Show"

If you are doing a "right and wrong" show, you must be especially careful in choosing the clothes for it. The last thing a buyer can tolerate, and rightly so, is to hear derogatory remarks about her merchandise. The emphasis in the "right and wrong" show must always be upon the idea that even the best clothes may look wrong on one person but very right on another. Wise selection can transform a mediocre, badly dressed woman into a chic, distinctive looking person. The "right and wrong" show uses the same clothes to create a bad effect on one model and a good effect on another model. Put the most attractive dress with a bouffant or pleated skirt on a woman with wide hips and you get an exaggeration of her figure defect. Add to this dress a hat which is flat and broad, and handbag and gloves that contrast sharply in color with the dress, and you have a perfect example of what the short stocky woman should *not* choose, when she goes shopping for her new spring outfit. Take the same dress, hat, bag and gloves and put them on a tall, slender woman, and the result is startlingly smart. No adverse reflections have been made about the merchandise, but a valuable lesson in clothes selection has been given. So for every point to be made, great care must be used in deciding what things will be most suitable.

Merchandise for the Conservative Woman of Means

In preparing a show for women of conservative tastes in the upper income brackets, excellence in quality will be the characteristic to be brought out in all the merchandise. For younger women at the same income level, designer originals, stunning and daring, can be shown. Whatever the customer group, the clothes must be chosen to appeal specifically to them if there is to be resulting business in the ready-to-wear and accessory departments.

Chapter 6

When Shall the Show Be Given?

The word "timing" is one of those staples in a retailer's vocabulary that pops up a dozen times a day. Timing is a big factor in placing orders; timing is all-important in planning advertising; timing is equally important in planning a fashion show.

There are many "times" which must be thought about — the time of year when your customers respond to shows, the days of the week when you can draw the largest audiences, the time of day best suited for a particular show.

The Best Time of Year

When considering the times of the year most suitable for shows, it is not enough to say in an off-hand manner, "Oh, spring and fall, of course." Spring and fall are long seasons, and which part of each will be best for a fashion show or for several shows will depend upon the customs and habits of the people to whom the show is directed. If you are planning a college show as part of your "Back to School" promotion, you must find out the habits of the majority of college girls in your trading area and the opening dates of the schools which most of them attend. If most girls go to schools which open late in September or early in October, and if the students, consequently, do not return from vacations until after Labor Day, then the show should obviously be held soon after their return. In some localities, however, the colleges open early in September, so the entire promotion, with its fashion show, should start around August 1.

The date of Easter has much to do with the timing of spring fashion shows, so that ordinarily it is good to have the spring previews about six weeks before the traditional "new-outfit day." If Easter is very late and the season is prematurely warm, however, it may be expedient to give the spring fashion show much earlier. Another circumstance making it advisable to allow a longer shopping period between the spring show and Easter is when business is slow and the fashion show may serve to whet customers' appetites for new clothes.

Spring and fall are not the only times of year for fashion shows. Resort wear shows are very popular and profitable, if they are timed correctly. Depending upon the customs of winter vacationers, such a show can be given either late in November or between Christmas and New Year's. When it comes earlier, there may be some fear that the show will interfere with Christmas business. This difficulty can be overcome easily, however, by combining the two ideas. An evening show for men and women can present clothes for both warm and cold resorts, and it can also highlight all the unusual gifts appropriate for those contemplating a winter vacation. Expensive sports equipment, fine luggage and all sorts of personal accessories rarely suitable for the average show can be highlighted. This can be the occasion for introducing the store's corps of personal shoppers, trained to give assistance with Christmas shopping problems and ready to take orders then and there.

Many fashion shows are given in advance of important social activities and events, such as the Kentucky Derby, the New York Horse Show, the opening of the Metropolitan Opera season, the opening of the opera in Dallas, and San Francisco, the beginning of the symphony seasons in many cities, the Mardi Gras in New Orleans. Here, the primary requisite is to have the show far enough in advance of the event, *before* people have purchased their clothes for the festivities. Many a fine show, timed too late for such an occasion, has drawn an interested audience but has failed to sell merchandise.

No season of the year provides greater varieties than does

the summertime, but again, these shows must be most carefully timed. Travel shows, aimed at business people, can be given as soon as the weather turns really warm and the store's stocks are at their peaks. Much vacation shopping is done during noon hours and evening shopping hours, so shows must be far enough in advance of vacation times to allow ample time for gathering the required wardrobe. Playtime shows, accenting beach, riding and other kinds of relaxation clothes, can be given early in May in preparation for the first big outdoor holiday, Decoration Day. Then, of course, there are the graduation shows which must be timed to coincide with the dates of these events in different places. In the East, graduations generally come at the end of June, so these shows can be given the first of June; but in the Middle West, graduations are mostly in the first week of June, necessitating giving the shows in early May. Always, the essential thing in determining the time of year for a show will be the habits and customs of the locality; also primary is the matter of allowing enough time for the customers to buy after the show and yet before the event for which it is being given.

The show being given for a special group, like high school students or career girls, requires still further analysis, in order that the time selected will not conflict with some school or business situation which would prevent people from attending. Certain times of the month are so busy in some offices that the workers have no time for outside activities. Certain periods in schools are devoted to examinations or school events, which would make it impossible for students to go to a fashion show. Whenever possible, it is a fine idea to consult with some of the people concerned about the timing of the show, to avoid the disappointment and loss of business which results from a conflict of this sort.

The Best Day

After you have made sure about the best time of year and that your show will not conflict with other events, you have to think about the best day of the week for the show. In some places, it is much better to have a show early in the week, on Tuesday or Wednesday; for these are places where week-ends loom large, and people start planning for them as early as Thursday. Great metropolitan centers have "week-enditis," and late-week fashion shows run the risk of not drawing good crowds. In other localities, the end of the week is excellent for fashion shows. Here, people are accustomed to shopping on Fridays and Saturdays, so a show on Thursday or even Friday will bring good results. Although Saturday shows, except for students and teachers, are usually discouraged, they may be given once in a while for a group from out-of-town who can come only on that day. On the other hand, no housewife will ever attend a show for herself on Saturday, for very clear reasons.

The Best Time of Day

Finally, there is the question of the time of day for the show, and, once again, the answer lies in an understanding of the habits and obligations of the audience. A fashion show for mothers of school children should preferably be given at a time when the children are in school. It must also be timed to allow for an ample shopping period after the show. Sometimes, the morning is the best time; in other cases, one-thirty in the afternoon is very satisfactory. No show for mothers should be given so late that the audience cannot get home in time to attend to the late-afternoon duties of a household.

Just as the show for mothers must be timed early in the day, so the show for the business woman must be held late in the day, usually around five-fifteen, even though this hour places a burden upon every person involved in the store. Of course, if the store is open one night a week, then that evening, around six-thirty, is ideal for the career girl show. Shows for teachers can be given at this hour, as well.

Often it is better to give a teen-age show after school, at four-thirty on a weekday, rather than on Saturday, especially if boys are to model, for many boys have Saturday jobs to prevent their modeling and to prevent their attending the show.

42

For the high fashion group, there are not such rigid time limitations; the type show will determine the time of day at which it is to be presented. The luncheon show is well-planned for one o'clock; the cocktail show for four o'clock; and the designer's show for late morning or mid-afternoon. When a spectacular evening show is to be given, it should generally be at eight-thirty.

Seasonal fashion parades and shows for older women should be held at two or two-thirty; and pattern shows, where the aim is to use the services of the visiting stylist to the greatest advantage, can be given on a two- or three-a-day basis to catch as many people as possible: ten-thirty, noon and two-thirty, or twelve, two-thirty and four o'clock.

Chapter 7

Where Shall the Show Be Held?

When the question, "Where shall we give our fashion show?" is asked, someone will come up immediately with, "On the ready-to-wear floor, of course." "Oh no," someone else will say, "Heaven protect us from the mess of a fashion show on the selling floor. Let's have it in the auditorium." Another person will ask, "How about having this one in the tea room?" Still another, "We should get the whole thing out of the store, and give it in the Colossal Hotel."

Giving the Show in the Store

All these suggestions represent important aspects of the question, the first of which is whether or not the show should be given in the store. It is fairly clear that it is generally best to have the fashion show somewhere within the four walls of the store. If the show does little more than bring traffic into the store (and, of course, it does much more), it has served the purpose of exposing customers to the goods on the store's counters. The show is given to make people want new things and having it in the store makes it easy for people to buy what the show has made them want. The idea of making it easy for people to buy is well understood by stores having flourishing custom-made salons. When these salons present their collections, the salespeople act as hostesses and stay with their regular customers, ready to take an order the moment the customer shows an inclination for a specific costume. While this method cannot be used for large shows in department stores, it is well to remember that much buying of fashion mer-

45

chandise is done under the stimulus of the moment. If that stimulus is allowed to lose its force, because it takes effort to find the merchandise, there will be a loss in sales.

Where, then, in the store shall the show be given? On the theory that the best place for a show is as close as possible to the goods you want to sell, the best place is the selling floor. A number of other matters, however, may overweigh this one big advantage. The awful upheaval that occurs in a crowded department, when a space must be made for the runway and the audience; the crowding of merchandise into stock rooms and racks; the loss of efficiency of salespeople due to the excitement caused by these preparations; the virtual halting of business long before and after the show—all are powerful reasons for considering long and carefully, before deciding to have a show on the selling floor. When the store is very spacious, however, and there is ample room for runways, dressing rooms, chairs for the audience and for displaying and selling the stock easily, then a show on the floor may be most satisfactory. The show on the floor will have to be a parade of fashions, for little dramatizing is possible under these conditions. The show on the floor is a wonderful way of infusing life into a department's lagging business, but it must be done with verve and enthusiasm, so that the customers will buy immediately. The buyer should brief her salespeople carefully about how to handle the rush of business after such a performance, and she should have enough salespeople so that customers will not be kept waiting too long.

It is always good to have a pattern show in the yard goods department, if it is at all possible. The wardrobes for the home sewer prepared and shown by various pattern companies are very inspiring to the woman who makes her own clothes. As she watches the show and identifies heself with some of the garments, she is also aware of all the intriguing fabrics that surround her. With her cleverly arranged program, on which she has checked those numbers she likes best, she can go immediately to the pattern counter, purchase her favorites, and buy the required materials without any effort.

Once in a great while, the store wishes to attract both men and women by giving an extravagant fashion revue, designed to publicize the fashion division and to heighten the store's fashion prestige. One such show utilized the entire ready-to-wear floor by putting up a runway which wound its way through all the departments—coats and suits, better dresses, millinery, sportswear, college shop. Since the plan of the floor made three main divisions, the chairs were grouped so that there were three audiences. Three commentators, placed so that they would not interfere with each other, explained the costumes which were passing before them. In this way, about fifteen hundred people saw the same show—a much larger number than could have been accommodated in the store's auditorium. Glamorous clothes, Powers models, several famous screen stars furnished the powerful appeal of this show. It resulted in unprecedented sales of expensive merchandise, including furs and jewels. Since such a show stops all normal business completely, it must be held in the evening. The enormous amount of work required to set it up makes this sort of presentation a "once-in-every-five-years" affair.

If the store has an auditorium or a space where fashion shows can be prepared and given without disturbing the routine of the selling floor, it is advisable to use it for the majority of the performances. A stage where settings can be changed and the curtain can be pulled, a good runway, opportunity to use lighting effects, adequate dressing rooms, a permanent public address system, and seats that are comfortable and enable the audience to see everything make the tasks of giving a show immeasurably easier. They make it possible for the fashion department to produce a real show that will accomplish the maximum returns. No makeshift place can equal in any respects an auditorium especially designed and equipped for giving fashion shows and other promotional events.

While the auditorium or hall is rarely close to the ready-to-wear floor, this handicap can be overcome in several ways. Probably the simplest and easiest of these is to make arrangements to have the elevator starter on the main floor, at a given signal, send enough empty elevators to the auditorium floor to carry the fashion show audience directly to the ready-to-wear floor. This device, if properly planned, is entirely successful. Another way to get people from the auditorium to a selling floor is to give them cards which, when presented in the proper department, will be redeemed with a favor of the fashion show. Introducing top-notch salespeople at the end of the show and announcing that these people will be ready to help customers with their clothes problems in specified departments, also causes customers to shop immediately after the show.

Some stores, which do not have auditoriums, use their tearoom or restaurant for fashion shows. In such cases, permanent equipment, easy to set into place, can be built so the transformation from restaurant to hall can be made simply and quickly. Care must be taken to allow enough time for this change to be made, otherwise disturbing complications will result.

Giving the Show Outside the Store

Having the show away from the store is, at times, the only way it can be done. When the store's facilities are not adequate for a large fashion revue, it is best to use a hotel ballroom, a theatre or a country club for the affair. Under such circumstances, it is a good idea for the store to make a tie-up with a powerful organization in the community, which raises funds for some worthy cause. Such an organization will take over the job of securing an excellent, capacity audience, and the store can concentrate on producing a good show. The publicity value of helping a group to make money for a charitable cause is great, and the general public approval the store gains from an endeavor of this kind extends far beyond the limits of the membership of the organization. The store can also take practical steps to insure after-the-show visits to the store by giving each guest an invitation to call at a certain department to receive a memento of the occasion.

Stores often receive requests from women's clubs, churches

and schools to give fashion shows for special occasions they are planning. It is imperative that the store establish a policy, which will, of course, be part of its over-all public relations program, in regard to giving outside shows for organizations. The store can, for example, decide not to give any outside shows, except for one or two major charities during the year. On the other hand, many stores have found that providing shows for clubs, schools and churches is an excellent way to build goodwill for the entire store. When times are uncertain, such shows attract many customers who might not otherwise patronize the store.

The moment it becomes known, however, that a certain store will give fashion shows for organizations, the requests will come in in unbelievable numbers. Suddenly, the fashion department will discover that it could devote its entire time to running around the countryside giving fashion shows. The decision of which clubs will have shows and which will not cannot be made on the spur of the moment or haphazardly. Nothing can do a store more harm than to bestow its favors in one direction and refuse them in another. There must be some reasonable, sound basis for deciding, and the store must have enough leeway, so that it can select those groups where it feels the work will be worth the effort.

In trying to work out a satisfactory formula for selecting the right club audiences, some stores place great emphasis upon the number of people who will attend the show. Although the number of people who respond to any promotion is always important, it is sometimes not the most vital one, as far as club shows are concerned. A small club of influential women can sometimes bring more business into a store than can a large group. By placing this most delicate task in the hands of a single person, who is an expert in public relations, the store can save itself untold difficulties and be assured that the money expended in these shows will be put to the best use. This person, skilled in handling people, and guided by the store's policies, will use the fashion show as a means to extend the store's trading areas into outlying districts as well as among those groups which the store wishes to cultivate. This can be done in such a way that no one will feel abused or discriminated against.

The store which decides to use this method of building good-will and ready-to-wear business should use two or three of its regular models and the fashion coordinator for the shows. Cleverly devised pocket editions of the fashion story can be prepared for these small presentations which will bring very good results. In addition, the fashion coordinator must understand thoroughly the procedures of the store regarding the preparation of merchandise to be taken out of the premises. She must know when the deliveries go out for certain areas, so she can arrange with the receiving department to list and check out the clothes and accessories in plenty of time for them to be picked up without disrupting the delivery routine. She must notify the delivery not only that the clothes are to go out at a certain time, but also that they must be picked up again at a given time. This one matter of delivery and pick-up of fashion show merchandise can either be orderly and smooth, or it can be a miserably irritating affair for everyone.

The fashion coordinator must realize that everything, down to the last pin, must be planned for, when she is taking a show out of the store. These shows are often held in halls, churches or schools where there are no facilities whatever. To make the job simpler, a questionnaire should be sent to the organization for which the show is to be given, so that as many arrangements as possible can be made by the club and so that the fashion person will know a little about what she'll be meeting. A possible set of such questions, which should be mimeographed for extensive use, follows:

(1) Is there a room large enough for four people to dress in?
(2) How close is this room to the place where the show will be given?
(3) Is a full-length mirror available?
(4) Can you provide several smaller mirrors?
(5) Will you provide an iron and ironing board?

(6) What size is the room where the show will be given?

(7) Is there a platform at the front of the room?

(8) If not, will you provide one about 12 inches high and at least 4 feet square?

(9) How many people do you expect to attend?

If there are no mirrors and the club cannot provide them, the store must send one; and so with all the other necessaries, they must be provided in one way or another.

Whenever it is possible, it is most satisfactory to transport the clothes in a regular clothes cage, in which all the apparel, after it has been pressed, can hang free. On the bottom can stand the boxes of hats, shoes, millinery and other accessories. These cages can be locked and, consequently, can be delivered before the show at the most convenient time for the delivery department. Two things of the utmost moment, however, must be remembered about these cages: first, the club must be notified, so that someone will be at the meeting place to receive the clothes cage; and second, the fashion coordinator must be sure to take along the key to the cage. Dire consequences can result from failure to do either of these things.

Schools are very eager for fashion assistance from department stores. Shows given for teen-agers in the store serve the schools in the immediate vicinity, but schools in outlying towns or country districts cannot participate in the store shows. Since a part of the home economics curriculum of most high schools deals with problems of grooming and dress, there is a fine opportunity for a progressive store to cultivate new customers by having someone go to these schools and give a good talk on grooming and the wise selection of clothes. In preparation for such an appearance, the store representative writes the home economics teacher that she will need four models—one size 10, two size 12, one size 14. She further specifies that they be of average height, have no glaring figure problems, and make a good appearance. She must also warn the teacher to tell the girls chosen that, in the event the clothes don't fit or are not becoming, someone else will have to do the modeling. In consultation with the teen-age buyer, the store representative selects six or eight outfits and accessorizes them. To allow for the fact that she has not seen her models, she takes along some extra accessories, so that any problems can most likely be solved. Time for fitting the models and coaching them in their parts must be allowed, so the store representative should arrive at least an hour in advance. That hour will be a busy one, but it is amazing to discover how eagerly the girls respond to the challenge of such a hastily arranged show, and how very creditably they acquit themselves.

The effect of such a performance upon the entire student body, and upon the teachers and mothers who are sometimes present, is enormous. Many times all the clothes are sold, then and there; and often parents and children who have never been in the store before become customers, visiting the store occasionally and using the mail order service extensively. The same kind of service is provided for college organizations, especially when the store is anxious to develop an untapped area of business. Numerous variations of this scheme can be used, according to the requirements of an individual store. This phase of the store's fashion program can be carried on by one person, if she has ingenuity and uses real showmanship.

"Where shall we give the fashion show?" Where it will do the store the greatest amount of good for the money expended.

Chapter 8

How Much Shall the Show Cost?

This question, "How much shall the show cost?" is one of the most difficult of all to answer. It is a question, however, of which every fashion coordinator should be most seriously aware, for knowledge of costs is always essential in merchandising. Too often, fashion people, who are really "show" people, people with creative imaginations and flairs, do not know as many of the hard, realistic facts about money as they should.

The best—although sometimes hampering—basis upon which the fashion department should operate is on the budget basis, just as do other departments of the store. Some stores consider fashion shows, however, as part of the over-all promotional activity and charge the expense to promotion. Thus the publicity director, the sales promotion director, or the advertising manager (as the case may be) exercises a kind of loose control over the fashion show expenditures of the store, and the fashion coordinator is never quite certain how far she can go with a show.

Making up a fashion show budget for a six-month or year period, as a separate item of publicity expense, while difficult, can regulate the expenditures and can assure an intelligent distribution of available money among the shows the store intends to give during the year. Producing a fashion show on a budget necessitates a constant and salutary check on expenses; it gives an accurate picture of how and for what the money was spent; and it serves as an excellent record for future reference.

Model Expenses

Exclusive of the salaries of the fashion coordinator and her assistant or assistants, there are a number of things—models' and dressers' fees, music, settings, and so on — for which money must be spent every time a show is presented. Models' fees must be paid for the time spent in fitting for the show, for rehearsals and for the performance. This is one place where fashion show costs can mount with dizzying rapidity, if proper preparations have not been made. When models have to wait around until the fashion department collects itself, when they have to try on clothes endlessly before the right ones are found, when the rehearsal is late by an hour in starting, the fashion show, which may have been planned as a modest little affair, can become a most expensive one. The clock ticks on inexorably, and every minute means money wasted under such conditions. Good planning cuts down these time-lags immeasurably. Having determined in advance what clothes are to be included and having also made some notes about what model could wear which outfit, the fashion coordinator can do the fittings with speed and accuracy. She will also set up a time schedule for fittings and adhere to it rigidly. The same procedure will be used for rehearsals, so that they start promptly and last only as long as is absolutely necessary to assure the success of the show.

The most satisfactory way of handling models for teen-age shows is to pay them an hourly wage, just as adult models are paid. When young people are paid in cash, instead of in merchandise, as some stores do, they have a greater sense of responsibility toward the project and their juvenile high spirits can be controlled much better. When stores furnish shows for clubs which, in turn, provide the models, it has no financial obligation. It may, or may not, according to its pleasure, present these amateur models with some small merchandise gift.

Dressers' Fee

The next set expense for the fashion show is the wages for the dressers. It is possible to find a number of young women within the store organization who can be trained to be efficient dressers. They are not only glad to earn the extra money, but also they usually enjoy being part of a show. Waitresses in the store's tearoom often make good dressers, and their schedules permit their doing this extra work. Girls in stock rooms or at service desks also can be called upon. Having trained dressers who are regular employees, simplifies the work of the fashion department immensely. It also reduces this expense item, for once they have learned the routines, dressers need be present only for the dress rehearsal and the performance.

Settings Expense

Other time and labor charges which can run the expense of a fashion show up like a fever thermometer are those resulting from having special settings and displays requiring the services of the carpenter and display departments. It is one thing to dream up a wonderful idea for a setting, and quite another to translate that dream into actual props. Carpenters are highly paid, skilled workers; the bill for some "little" thing may be out of all proportion to its importance. After careful consultation with the head carpenter and the display manager, an idea may have to be discarded because it would be too expensive to execute. Whatever is decided upon in the way of settings and decorations should be started well in advance of the show, so that the work can be fitted into the regular schedules of the carpenter shop and the display department. Last minute ideas, requiring overtime work for which carpenters are paid time and a half and sometimes double time, can throw the entire budget off balance for months to come.

Alteration and Pressing Costs

Another essential item that can be very costly unless it is understood and controlled is the alteration and pressing expense of the show. An experienced fashion expert chooses her models so they can wear stock sizes, thus almost eliminating the necessity for alterations. Hemlines, of course, often have to be evened; except for the most unusual cases, however, no clothes should be chosen that need extensive alterations. Not only does this work cost money, but also the garment cannot be sold at the full mark-up after alterations have been made.

Pressing the garments for a show cannot and should not be slighted or avoided. Every model must be perfectly groomed when she steps upon the runway; her garments must be without a wrinkle; they must look immaculate and hang flawlessly. This effect can be produced only if the garments have been meticulously pressed a short time before the show begins. Understanding the alteration department's problems and advance planning can again reduce the expense of pressing. When the alteration head is notified long enough in advance and is given the clothes in time, he can work this job into his schedule. It takes time, lots of it, to press forty or fifty garments; and if they are rushed in to be done at the last minute, pressers will have to work overtime, at time and a half, to complete the work. The result—another enormous labor charge!

Service Charges

The place where the show is held, whether it be on the floor or in the auditorium, must be set up for the occasion and cleaned up afterwards. This means a charge for porters' services, which must be included as an item of show expense. Then it is wise to have an electrician on duty to operate the lights and to regulate the microphone—another item of expense.

Music Fees

Every show must have some sort of musical background. Here there is room for some leeway, for one or two musicians may be all that are needed for certain shows. For a high school show, an accordionist or a juke box may suffice. For a very elaborate production, a string ensemble or a small orchestra may be deemed necessary. Whatever it may be, there must be provision in the budget for music for the show.

Promotion Expenses

Last of all, every show must be promoted, if it is to be successful. This is such an important item of expense that it must receive separate consideration, but such items as publicity photographs, entertainment of the press, direct mail pieces, newspaper advertising, posters, programs and other promotional aids are classified under promotion.

In addition to all these expenses which are an inseparable part of the show, the budget should provide a sum to be used, as seems most advantageous, for occasional out-of-town models, special decorations and favors, and strictly fashion show merchandise.

Chapter 9

How Shall the Fashion Show Be Promoted?

Letting customers know that there is to be a fashion show is essential, of course; and there are numerous ways of doing so: through newspaper advertising, through invitations sent directly to customers, through unpaid publicity and through radio spot announcements and sometimes a radio interview. As in all other phases of show production, the promotion of the show must be planned carefully and far enough ahead to permit its being done most effectively; and the cost must be controlled, so that it is, like all other promotion, commensurate with the returns.

Determining how much money to spend on promoting a given show is very difficult, because it is very hard to measure the results in dollars and cents and because, to a great extent, the value of the show lies in that intangible realm of goodwill building. The show, in this respect, is like institutional advertising which benefits the entire store but cannot be gauged exactly in its effect. The immediate objective of advertising the show is, to be sure, very practical indeed; it is to assure a capacity attendance. How much or how little it takes to achieve this varies in different places and at different times. It is safe to say that all means of publicizing the show, which do not cost money, should be employed; and paid methods should be used according to the best judgment regarding the requirements of each show.

Invitations

The first matter to be decided, because it takes the most time to prepare, is whether or not to send individual invitations to cus-

59

Informal Invitation

to a fashion clinic for mature women

DEAR CUSTOMER:

Can you set aside three afternoons—Monday, Wednesday and Thursday, March 9, 11 and 12—from 2:30 to 3:30, to attend to some very personal and important business?

Because a number of our customers have expressed much interest in the idea, we are planning a series of fashion clinics designed especially for the mature woman. During these three sessions, we shall consider very informally, but we hope most enjoyably, many of the puzzling problems of clothing selection for the mature figure. Although we shall give a fashion show each time, it won't be the ordinary one, for we intend to discuss most carefully such things as diet, exercise, selecting the proper foundation garment, choosing the most becoming hat for various facial types, determining what lines and designs, as well as fabrics, are most suitable for various figures and many other equally important matters.

We know that many women will want to attend these sessions, so we would like very much to hear from you as soon as possible, so that we can make your reservation, to assure you a place in our auditorium. The nominal fee of $1.50 can be charged to your account. Just fill in the enclosed, self-addressed card today and return it to us promptly.

We are looking forward to seeing you at our first Fashion Clinic.

Sincerely yours,

THE JAMES J. BLANK COMPANY

How Shall The Fashion Show Be Promoted?

Formal Invitations

should be printed or engraved on fine card stock, depending upon the elaborateness of the occasion.

THE JAMES J. BLANK COMPANY

requests

the pleasure of your company at a

Fashion Show and Cocktail Party

WEDNESDAY AFTERNOON, OCTOBER 11, 19 , AT FOUR THIRTY

TERRACE TEA ROOM, SEVENTH FLOOR

R.S.V.P.

You are cordially invited to attend

"A Spring Fantasy"

A dramatic presentation of spring fashion highlights

to be held on

WEDNESDAY, MARCH 8, 19 , AT ONE O'CLOCK

TERRACE TEA ROOM

THE JAMES J. BLANK COMPANY

Luncheon $2.00   Reservations: CI. 3000

---

tomers. When the show is being planned to appeal to a special audience, which has never before received such attention, it is a good idea to send invitations to a carefully selected list of people. This invitation should be written in a friendly, informal manner. Also, when the store is to have a showing of some designer's collection or when it is giving an elaborate fashion luncheon, tea or cocktail party, it should use formal, elegant invitations, often requiring a response from the recipient. For all other shows, it is usually unnecessary to send personal invitations.

Newspaper Advertising

Newspaper advertising should probably begin about a week in advance of the show. The first announcement can be included in the store's fashion ads and can be distinguished from the merchandise by putting it into a box and using an invitation-like layout. During that week, every ready-to-wear and accessory ad should carry either a similar box ad or a line reminder about the show on such and such a date. The line reminder is especially valuable, for it costs practically nothing and it keeps the show constantly before the readers of the fashion ads. If it is deemed wise, a separate ad about the show can be used in the papers the night before and on the morning of the show.

Although the advertising department does the actual layout and copywriting for the fashion show ads, the fashion coordinator has the duty of making the arrangements for the advertising and for furnishing the ideas for the copy. It is she who has created the theme for the show; it is she who must furnish the copywriter with the inspiration and enthusiasm to do an outstanding job on the show's advertising.

Newspaper Publicity

The fashion show provides the store one of its best opportunities to obtain free publicity in the newspapers, something for which every store is constantly hoping and searching. Without going into the psychological reasons why even a short notice in the editorial columns of a newspaper can bring such remarkable reactions in customers, it is sufficient to point out that this fact makes it imperative that every publicity aspect of the show be exploited to the fullest extent. To do this successfully, the fashion person must realize, first of all, that newspapers are interested and will accept *only* newsworthy stories for their editorial columns. It is news, of course, that The Blank Company will present a fashion show. A story written around this fact, with some information about the clothes to be shown, may get a half inch of space in some obscure corner of the paper, chiefly as an acknowledgment that the store has bought space to advertise the show. Some people will see the little notice, but the store will have gained practically nothing in return for the time spent in sending the item to the paper.

The smart woman, with a genuinely promotional approach to her merchandise, will scan her show to find some angle that will make real news, the kind women want to read and will remember. This must be done long enough ahead to allow for proper preparation and placing of the material. All newspapers recognize the interest of their readers in fashion news; many have fashion editors because of this interest. They will therefore welcome an excellent photograph of some unusual costume in the show and a well-written article about the entire project. Sometimes, photographs can be obtained from manufacturers, but most often, if it has been decided to go to this expense, the store has the photographs made either by an outside fashion photographer or by its own photography department. Once in a while, the newspaper will make the photograph, depending upon the requirements and assignments of its fashion editor. If the store prepares the photographs, they should be made at least a week and preferably ten days before the show. This gives time for finishing them well and for writing the release to accompany each one.

In writing the release, it is always necessary to point out the most distinguishing characteristic of the costume in the photograph and also to include facts about the show in the first sentence. The following will give an idea of how the first sentence should be expressed:

"The bloused jacket, with emphasis upon wide shoulder and sleeve treatment, and the pencil-slim skirt of this pin-check navy and white suit, will emphasize one of the season's most interesting fashion trends when it is shown on Wednesday, March 8, at 1:00 in 'A Spring Fantasy,' the fashion show to be presented by the J. J. Blank Company."

The remainder of the story will give other interesting fashion news, calculated to arouse the reader's desire to see the show. Such stories help to build the store's reputation as a fashion leader, as well as accomplishing the more immediate purpose of bringing women to the show. When releases are to be prepared for more than one paper, and there must be a separate one for each publication in the city, a different photograph must be used for each release. Competing papers will not publish the same picture nor use the identical story.

Press Showings

The fashion show publicity release sent to the fashion editors of the town's papers may often result in satisfactory advance coverage for the show. It may not, however, get as much free publicity for the store as the show deserves. One of the best ways of assuring ample coverage is to have an advance press showing of some of the most stunning and unusual ensembles to be presented in the show. A small luncheon in a secluded spot, a cocktail party in the fashion office, or sometimes even an afternoon or morning press meeting may be used to show these costumes to the press. Releases should be ready to give to the fashion editors, for they will welcome the help such material gives them. Such an informal affair will often result in the publication of the release as an advance story and a follow-up immediately after the show written by the fashion editors. Thus the store receives double mention in the editorial columns of the newspapers.

If the show is featuring some unusual personalities, or if the idea for the show is very new and sufficiently dramatic, these facts can be used to highlight the publicity. Guests of prominence can also be interviewed on the radio, very often without charge to the store. Local radio stations, which sell time to stores for many commercial broadcasts, are glad to provide time, usually fifteen minutes, for an interview of a fashion celebrity by the fashion coordinator or some other well-known store executive. The script for such an interview should be prepared by the store and mention of the forthcoming show should be worked in skillfully. Many women who would otherwise overlook the show hear such broadcasts and are not only impressed with the store's fashion leadership, but also attend the performance as well.

Trade Publicity

One kind of far-reaching publicity which is sometimes overlooked in the rush of preparing a show is the story that can be sent to trade papers and journals. The show packed with good ideas will always provide a story of interest to the editors of trade publications. This publicity will not have an effect upon the store's customers, but it will add to the store's prestige among its business associates. It is another way of publicizing the store's accomplishments over a very wide area without any expenditure of money.

These are the conventional methods of securing publicity for a fashion show. There are other ways of extracting publicity from a show which can be seized upon by the creative, alert publicity person. They depend upon local conditions and cannot be specifically enumerated, but to the trained eye they are available and should be exploited to the greatest possible degree in the best interests of the store.

Chapter 10

Where Do Ideas for Fashion Shows Come From?

All around us, in everything we and our customers do — from the commonplace to the most exciting occurrences in life — are ideas for fashion shows. It takes genuine curiosity and interest in people, as well as accurate knowledge about them, however, to translate vague generalities into concrete fashion show ideas or themes.

People's lives move in fairly regular cycles, so every year, as surely as spring comes, as certainly as fall winds blow, stores show clothes for these seasons. Every year, people are married; they have babies; they grow older; they go on vacations. For all these activities, their clothing needs recur with predictable certainty. There is nothing new or different about having a bridal show, or a vacation show, or a travel show, yet all these old, familiar shows can be decked out in fresh, new themes that seize upon current interests and events and thus catch the public fancy.

Working Out the Theme

In working out a theme for a fashion show, the fashion expert, like the display director, has her most satisfying, artistic experience. Nothing is more rewarding for her than to hit upon a delightfully new approach that can spark the advertising of the fashion departments, provide splendid interior and exterior display possibilities and make the show itself something for the customers to talk about.

To arrive at that wonderful theme, the fashion director may

spend several sleepless nights and a good many nerve-racking daylight hours. She will be mulling over many things; she will be drawing upon her fund of knowledge for the right, the perfect way of formulating her show of the moment. The fund of knowledge upon which she draws is not merely technical information that she has gathered during her business career; if she is wise, however, she constantly watches and clips all the trade journals recording ideas that have been tried and proved by other stores. The successful fashion person must be awake and alive to her entire world. She must know books and music; she must be informed about the theater, the movies, the radio, television and the new "just on the horizon" things. She must read fashion magazines constantly and widely; she must know her fashion history, as well as contemporary fashion. She must visit art galleries and museums; she must keep abreast of all the astounding innovations constantly being introduced in all phases of our culture. She must live continuously in a general atmosphere of idea-production.

The creative fashion leader must realize, above all, that for every *workable* idea she produces, she'll probably think up a dozen impractical ones. She must learn to discard the impractical ideas without regret, and keep sternly in search of a concept which will fire the enthusiasms of others and also meet the rigid requirements of her budget and the limitations of her work situation. Just being able to think up some clever theme for a show is not nearly enough in this business. You have to see how you can translate that "clever" idea into tangibles, before you can grow very excited about it. Knowing thoroughly all the so-called "ropes" of fashion show production is the only avenue through which ideas can be successfully harnessed to reality.

Bridal Shows

Each year, the fashion director must find new ways of presenting her bridal shows. Last year, let us say, her early spring show was entitled **QUEEN OF HEARTS.** In that show the first scene presented the bridal party, and subsequent scenes showed the bride as "Queen of the Kitchen," "Queen of the House," "Queen of the Day," and "Queen of the Ball."

This year, the trend indicates that bridal customers are more money-conscious than they were last year. Therefore, the theme **LOVE ON A BUDGET** is adopted. Here, every phase of the trousseau, as well as the wedding and attendants' dresses, are presented from the point of view of value in relation to price. Great attention is paid to the coordination of the trousseau to secure the maximum versatility. Changes of accessories to create different effects for different occasions are emphasized. The advisability of selecting a basic color for the wardrobe and then building around that color is brought out. The wedding dress is a convertible one that can become an evening dress or dinner gown afterwards. Programs are little budget books and the stage background is a huge budget book with the show theme in gold letters to give a decorative touch. Departmental displays, store posters and newspaper advertising carry out the same idea.

A quotation from the marriage ceremony can also be used as a bridal show theme. **FROM THIS DAY FORTH** can be interpreted in several ways. For instance, the show can open with the altar scene. Successive scenes will develop the various phases of young married life such as "Fun in the Kitchen," where you could show casual indoor clothes; "Before the Fireplace," presenting lounge and informal wear; "Stepping Out," for showing suits, coats and dresses; "Putting Your Best Foot Forward," for cocktail and evening clothes. This is just one of a number of ways in which such a theme can be worked out.

One store decided that it would be valuable for its customers to show bridal gowns and trousseaus for different types of brides —the tall ones, the short ones, medium height—and also for those who like fluffy, elaborate things and those who prefer the simpler styles. Each section of the show, therefore, was devoted to one type giving a rounded picture of the season's fashions appealing to different tastes. This show proved highly successful, for it made the audience realize that the store was aware of the preferences of its customers and was prepared to provide exactly what each desired.

Another store combined household information with the showing of clothes for the bride. This provided an opportunity, of course, to show other kinds of merchandise, but primarily the idea was to give valuable bits of information which are so greatly needed by the newly married housewife.

The Spring Show

Weariness with winter's cold makes women eager to learn about spring's fashion picture. So, while snow and slush may still be on the ground, the first spring fashions can make their debut. **SWINGING INTO SPRING** was the caption of an outstanding spring show. On the stage were three garland-entwined swings in which sat three models as the curtain opened. Each model was dressed in one of that spring's most important colors. In turn, each one went down the runway followed by other models featuring the colors worn by the leader. For each successive scene, there were three models leading the group of clothes which was being presented.

THE SORCERY OF SPRING lends itself to a number of interpretations, among them the use of a top-hatted, black-clad magician to introduce each part of the show. Such sub-titles as: "Magic in Suits," "Sleight-of-hand Separates," "Bewitched Evenings" can be used. The same title could be used in featuring the spring color, texture and line story by captioning its parts with "Magic in Texture," "Magic in Line," and "Magic in Color."

To exemplify the French influence, the Parisian flavor can be caught in such scenes as "Strolling Down the Boulevard," "The Sidewalk Cafe," "The Left Bank," and "Sous les Etoiles." A few simple props can suggest the continental atmosphere, and pink and white striped programs with a black line drawing of a sidewalk cafe makes an attractive program.

The Easter Parade provides a means of showing fashions for the whole family. A single backdrop, perhaps a stained-glass window flanked with palms, makes an appropriate setting. This is a show where fashions for men as well as women and children should be presented.

Other titles that may be developed for the spring show are: **BLUE PRINTS FOR SPRING, LILAC TIME, FASHIONS WITH A FUTURE.**

The Summer Show

The summer show, with its great diversity of color and style, is one of the most interesting of the entire year. This is the year's playtime for which people plan throughout the long winter months. It is the time when many conservative people throw caution to the winds and buy things they would not consider purchasing for other times of the year. The fashion director should join wholeheartedly in this joyous attitude and she should use her knowledge of her customers and her imagination to the fullest extent. Often, it is advisable to give a series of vacation shows, each one devoted to some particular kind of vacation. Certainly, the immense popularity of European travel deserves to be dealt with in a show all its own. For those who will travel by boat, there is one kind of fashion story to tell. The air travelers want other kinds of fashion information. The north woods beckon to some, while others will seek a seashore jaunt.

If the budget does not permit such an elaborate program, then a combined vacation show can be used. **TWO WEEKS WITH PAY** is a show which has become traditional for several stores and it appeals, of course, to a very large group of people. Considering all the varied desires of those who spend two weeks on vacation, this show can include: "Caribbean Cruise" for shipboard wardrobes; "Over the Housetops" for air travel ensembles; "Mountain Vistas" for a camping trip; "Washed by the Waves" for a seaside sojourn; "Down on the Farm" for a simple country rest and "Overland" for an auto journey. In each case, there should be a variety of clothes including what would be suitable for such a vacation. Since a sea voyage makes it possible to take a trunk, the clothes can obviously be more diversified and dressier than one would show for an airplane trip. Bouffant skirts, frilly blouses, elaborate evening clothes are fine for shipboard but completely impractical for air travel, where packability and versatility are the primary requirements. It is remarkable how eager customers are for the factual information about vacation wardrobes that can be submitted in a summer show. They need to be shown how to select and coordinate a wardrobe using a basic color around which to assemble all the necessary garments. They are anxious to see how this wardrobe can be made exciting and varied. They also want to hear the latest news about fabrics, especially those suitable for air journeys.

A show devoted entirely to the cruise idea was called **ALL ABOARD FOR FASHION.** The program design was the prow of a ship done in bright blue outlines on white. A simple backdrop of waves with a ship's railing and a roped gangplank from the runway to the stage gave the desired atmosphere. The five scenes were "All Aboard" featuring travel suits, coats and ensembles. Then came "Sports Time" with a shuffleboard game in progress and the showing of all sorts of play clothes and beach togs. "Grand Slam" showed the passengers in filmy afternoon and early evening dresses at bridge or sipping cocktails. "Petticoats and Party Gowns" showed both lingerie and evening gowns as the models prepared for the ship's ball. Last came "After Ball Is Over" displaying nightgowns, pajamas and lounging clothes.

FLOWER FANTASY can be the title of a summer show. In a six-scene show use the captions "Morning Glory" for robes and lingerie; "Water Lily" for bathing and beach wear; "Mountain Laurel" for casual daytime clothes; "Four O'Clock" for afternoon clothes; "Moonflower" for evening costumes, and "Orange Blossoms" for a wedding scene as climax of the show.

Current hit plays can always be an inspiration. The drama, **PICNIC** provided inspiration for several successful summer shows. Here the emphasis should be on all types of casual and play clothes, including gay and colorful separates for square dancing. One store served box lunches to its audience in connection with such a show.

Authentic objects of primitive art were exhibited in connection with a show entitled **SAFARI.** This travel show accented vivid colors and designs. Both the backdrop and the programs can carry out this idea in a number of ways.

The Fall Show

The fall show is a very important one on the fashion calendar, for here will be shown the clothes that represent the greatest outlay in money. Autumn is the time when fashions reflect the foreign influence, but it lays the foundations for much of the fashion information for the spring showings, as well.

MAGIC TOUCH FASHIONS can be the theme of such a show in which the accent should be on how the new styles lend a magic touch to the smart woman. The season's most vivid and flattering colors, its newest textures and its most striking lines should be highlighted. "Magic in Color" can present coats, suits, daytime dress and evening costumes notable for their color beauty. "Magic in Texture" brings the newest fabrics to the customers' attention, while "Magic in Line" gives new design features the spotlight. "The Magic Touch" can give many clever ideas in mixing, matching and accessorizing that customers are so eager to see.

Another approach to the fall fashion presentation can employ the art consciousness of customers. The **GREAT PAINTERS** theme has been used many times, but it never grows stale if it is interpreted in interesting ways. An entire show can be planned around one of the great masters like Rembrandt, or a group of painters like the Dutch School can be used. During the comprehensive exhibition of Van Gogh's works at the Metropolitan Museum in New York, several stores tied in with Van Gogh fashion shows featuring his striking shades and color combinations.

PICK OF THE CROP is a good autumn title linked to the harvest idea. Backdrop and programs can depict cornucopias spilling out brightly colored fruits, making an interesting way of pin-pointing color as the outstanding autumn fashion feature. "Vintage Tones" would accent all sorts of costumes in wine shades from burgundy to deep purples. "Cider and Doughnuts" would include the tawny shades and the browns, while "Evergreen Magic" would tell the green story.

Show Ideas for all Seasons

There are many ideas that can be adapted to all the seasons. They need only the application of some imagination and ingenuity to make them usable both for winter and summer, spring or fall.

FASHION HEADLINES is derived from the newspaper idea. For this, regardless of the time of year, a simple and effective backdrop is a simulated newspaper through whose pages the models step onto the stage. The six scenes for such a show might be: "Business News" for showing street wear; "Vacation News" for winter or summer resort clothes; "Theatre and Nightspots" for late-day and dressy clothes; "TV and Radio News" for lounge and at-home clothes, and "Brides in the News" for a wedding scene.

The theatrical or movie hits of a season can always serve as an interest-catching device for a fashion show. In **FOOTLIGHTS ON FASHION** each scene is given the name of a current hit. Here both backdrop and program should be done in black and white using the comic and tragic masks as the design. The scenes of one such show were: "Bus Stop" for daytime clothes; "Hatful of Rain" for rain wear; "Matchmaker" for telling the separates story; "My Fair Lady" for dressy clothes of all kinds; "Pipe Dream" for a wedding.

FASHION GOES INTERNATIONAL can spark a show which will give the customers knowledge of how fashion draws upon the entire world for its inspiration. The stunning United Nations building in New York can be sketched on both backdrop and program to lend a true international flavor. To introduce each scene, use a model dressed in an authentic costume of the country whose influence is best illustrated in the clothes that follow. The effect of oriental ideas on western fashion has been particularly striking, so a Chinese costume reveals the original of

74

the mandarin collar, the tight pants and other details of that influence. The richness of fabrics and the beautiful color combinations that have come to us from India will be exemplified in a Hindu sari. The national costumes of such countries as Norway, Austria and Italy have played a great part in shaping the designs of our separates. The list of nations to which we owe our thanks for the exciting variety of our clothes is about as wide as is the world. The public loves to see how the clever and imaginative U.S. designers have roamed the globe for inspiration.

The ideas for presenting the fashion story come out of the individual season itself or out of the things the store wishes to accomplish, so there is literally no limit to what can be done. So often, the color story is the outstanding thing in a season's clothes. One clever way of telling this was devised by The Fashion Group in New York City. Each of the six scenes was devoted to showing how all the shades of a color were being employed to give customers the greatest color varieties in clothes that had been available in years. To put this idea over, each scene was heralded by a page girl wearing a long black silk cape over simple black velvet pants and a white shirt. As the page stepped to the front of the stage, she opened her cape by extending her arms to shoulder height and revealed the cape's lining which ranged from the palest shades of a single color to the deepest hues. As the commentator explained about the many varieties of the color in fashion for that season, the page moved back still keeping her cape widespread, and models arrayed in the same colors appeared on the stage. At the end, all six pages—one each for the pinks to reds, the pale blues to navy, mauves to purple, lemon yellow to orange, off-white to deep beige, and black and white— came on stage and formed a dramatic and impressive closing for the show.

One enterprising specialty shop has experimented with great success with an idea that at first glance might seem impractical. This is the **YOUR SIZE** show. A full hour's show was devoted to each of the sizes 10, 12, 14, 16, and one for junior sizes and another for half-sizes. This an excellent way in which to show the public how wide the store's assortments are in all the wanted sizes. It can also attract many new customers who may not have been aware that the store stocked her particular size so extensively.

High School and College Shows

With the ever-increasing importance of the teen-age market, shows for high school and college students have achieved first-rank importance. If anything, such shows require even more imagination and ingenuity than do the presentations for adults. The young are eager to attend and participate but the shows must be clever and interesting to catch the attention of this youthful audience. Being intensely absorbed in themselves, teen-agers like shows that center around their lives and enthusiasms.

At a time when a high school fashion board was just being organized by one store and when the interest was still rather lukewarm, one enterprising fashion coordinator decided to use boys as well as girls for models. To handle the delicate matters of boy versus girl, she secured an equal number of boys and girls for the show. Then she put the names of the girls in a hat and let each boy draw for his partner. This mixed up the representatives of the various schools, which proved very good. The plan was to have all the modeling done in pairs so that the partners would in each case appear together on the runway. The show was in five scenes, all pertaining to phases of a high school student's life. "The First Bell" showed school clothes: "The Football Rush," outdoor wear; " 'Coke' Dates,"sweaters and matchmakers of all kinds; "Movie Time," suits, coats and dresses, and "Magic Moments" presented formals. This last required the boys to wear Tuxedos and there were groans and protests when the idea was first presented. By the time the show was given, however, the boys had discovered how much fun it is to dress up and, as a result, the show launched a considerable dress-up movement among the boys of that city.

FIRST IMPRESSIONS ARE EVERYTHING was the title of a college show that brought excellent results. "The First Day" gave opportunity for showing suits, coats and dresses; "The First Football Game" for jackets, slacks, cordoroys, and many other things; "The First Dorm Get-Together" showed lounging clothes, Bermuda shorts, and so on; "The First Storm" presented rain wear; "The First Tea," afternoon clothes; "The First Formal," evening gowns.

Special Events Shows

Many fashion shows are tied in with special events of local interest and derive their ideas from such local interest. Louisville, Kentucky, for instance, has the Derby each year and this city, as well as many surrounding it, use this event as an occasion for a fashion show. The Horse Show in New York, the opening of the opera in San Francisco, the 500 mile race in Indianapolis, the Mardi Gras in New Orleans, and countless other events all over the nation give the spark of uniqueness to fashion presentations.

So, out of everyday events, special occasions, out of people's lives, books, currently popular plays and movies, TV and radio, out of every aspect of experience, the alert, alive fashion director can create some concept by which she can tell the fashion story provocatively, excitingly and in a timely way.

Chapter 11

The Commentary: Who Shall Write It? Who Shall Deliver It?

Writing the Commentary

The script for the fashion show should *always* be written. This is the only way in which the fashion coordinator can be certain that she has included all the essential facts about the clothes and accessories which the audience must hear. It is the only way she can avoid repetitions that become monotonous and boring.

The first thing to be worked out is the introduction which will create the friendly atmosphere that should be apparent at every show and which will put the audience in the proper mood to enjoy and understand the show. Using the theme of the show as the central idea for the introduction, the script should emphasize the fact that the store is a fashion leader in the community; it brings its customers the newest, widest selections of fashion merchandise; it can be relied upon as a fashion authority; and it is proud to be able to educate and lead its customers in fashion matters. This cannot be said blatantly and without modesty; it must be framed in words which convey the meaning without exposing the store to the justified charge of being unduly conceited. Customers are exceedingly sensitive to exaggerated claims; they accept the idea of superiority only if it is demonstrated. To convey this message honestly and convincingly requires painstaking thought; it cannot be produced "off the cuff," unless the commentator has had vast experience. Writing the thoughts is the only way of assuring their clarity and correctness. In addition to these general ideas, the introduction should outline the season's fashion picture, and explain any other purposes for giving the show. These purposes include reasons for giving a career girl's show, a show for the older woman, one for housewives, and so on. With all that is to be included in the introduction, there may be a tendency to make it too long. This is always to be avoided, for people grow restless, if the curtain is too long in going up. The trick, then, is to say all that is necessary as briefly and enthusiastically as possible.

For each costume there must be some comments, comments which will point out the fashion features of both clothes and accessories and will relate them to the over-all fashion story. In doing this, there will necessarily be some repetition, but repetition is not to be feared if it is done skillfully. Repetition is essential, if the lessons of the show are to be driven home as they should be. The danger is that repetition will be monotonous, and this is one reason why the written script is so vital. The commentator has time, when she writes, to devise new ways of saying the same thing.

What about the length of the comments about each costume? No absolute rule can be given, but certainly the commentator who babbles on endlessly is irritating and ineffectual. There should definitely be some time, while a model is on the runway, when the commentator is silent and the audience can give their entire attention to the ensemble. During this silence, the commentator need not feel self-conscious, for no one is concerned with her at all; all are interested in the model. A good way to arrange the comments is to point out the highlights of the outfit as the model appears; then be silent while she walks to the end of the runway; and as she returns to the stage, point out the features of the accessories which should be noticed. On the last turn toward the audience from the stage, the commentator repeats the most important single point she wishes to emphasize.

If the show has changes of scenery, the fashion commentator has a chance before each curtain to talk about some special fashion idea or about some one department. Before a scene showing basic dresses with accessory changes, for example, she can speak briefly about the accessory colors most in vogue that season, or about the great versatility of the basic dress, because it can be accessorized in so many ways. She may discuss the newest hosiery shades or tell about striking new costume jewelry or scarfs. Before a scene presenting evening clothes, she can speak about the new hair styles and the latest make-up, giving the beauty salon and the cosmetics department special "plugs." An entire line of perfumes may be promoted in connection with a show with comments about the suitability of various fragrances at different times of day. Thus departments which sometimes feel slighted by the fashion department receive valuable mention. When a cosmetic and perfume line are included in a show, the manufacturer will often provide delightful favors for distribution to the audience.

The aim of the commentator should always be to give credit to as many departments as are represented in the show, without making such credits a bore. Adroitly including a reference to the housewares section, if a model in an attractive housedress happens to be carrying a new broom or other household article, often results in sales in that department after the show. Luggage carried by models deserves special mention, and sports equipment should always be pointed out.

And when is all this comment written? It will have to be put together in final form after the dress rehearsal, which often comes the night before the show. Much preliminary work can be done on it, however. The introduction can be written several days ahead; and during the fittings, notes can be made, on separate cards for each outfit, about striking aspects to be noted. As the costumes are accessorized, the hat, bag, etc. can also be noted on the card bearing the dress or suit information. By the time the fashion coordinator has fitted a show and has thought about it as constantly as she must, she knows a great deal about all the merchandise. Having created the idea for the show, she should not have too much trouble in putting all her information together. These cards, numbered in the sequence in which the models will appear, should be in the hands of the show director during the dress rehearsal, for there will inevitably be last-minute changes to be noted as soon as they are made.

Finally, after everything is set, the fashion coordinator takes all her data cards and rewrites one for each outfit, filling in any ideas which she needs to include. For this final task before the show, the commentator should insist upon absolute quiet and solitude, for she is not only rewriting her script, she is rehearsing for the show as well. This is her period of review of every detail, so that she can be certain that nothing has been overlooked and everything is correct. Too much emphasis cannot be given to this last, quiet, objective survey of the show, before it is exposed to public criticism.

Delivering the Commentary

Generally, the fashion coordinator does the commenting for the fashion show. She knows the fashion story best; she has created the show; she has written the commentary; she should present it to the public. This demands the ability to speak well in public, however, and many very capable fashion people know little about public speaking. One of the best investments that can be made, in such a case, is for some speech lessons. Those who have had some training, as well as those who have not, can nevertheless practice speech and can establish some speech habits which will always be valuable.

The first thing to understand and to put into constant practice is enunciating every syllable of each word. This will mean studying words to become certain of their syllables and to know exactly where the accents in words come. Every vowel and every consonant is enunciated in a unique way, a way which can be acquired only through study and practice. Many good books on speech have been written, all of which include simple exercises for mastering the enunciation of sounds. The serious person, who earnestly wants to do a better job with her fashion show comments, will invest in one of these books, if she cannot take the necessary lessons. The first precept for all public speakers is: *Speak clearly and distinctly.*

Giving every vowel and consonant its full value will immediately slow down the tempo of speech. It is essential to realize that all persons who use a language constantly develop a speed in speaking which often makes them hard to understand even in private conversation. They rush through their words at breakneck speed, hardly taking time for a breath, and much of what they have said is lost. The blurring effect of this haste in speaking is immeasurably magnified when an audience is being addressed and, consequently, no one beyond the second row can hear what is being said. The second precept for all public speakers is: *Speak slowly and deliberately.*

The next thing to strive for is variety of tone. Nothing dulls the attention of an audience more quickly than a monotone. People simply will not listen, if the voice of the commentator drones along at the same level, without variation, without life, without enthusiasm. How can anyone expect customers to become excited about merchandise, if the person who is talking about it seems to be bored to death with it? It is difficult to know whether or not the voice is a monotone, but having a recording of your voice made will reveal it very quickly. Then conscious effort to change the pitch frequently will begin to improve this speech defect. The third precept for all public speakers is: *Fill your speech with tone variations.*

Many people have the mistaken notion that a microphone can cure all speech defects. This is absurd, of course, for the microphone merely amplifies what is spoken into it. If the speech is blurred through lack of good enunciation, if it is too rapid, these things are amplified over the microphone and often made very much worse. A microphone is important in a show, nevertheless, for the commentator must speak over background music and this is difficult without the aid of an amplifier. Taking for granted that the commentator knows how to speak well, there are a few other matters which should be tested before the show. The first is to be certain that the microphone is set correctly, so the voice will reach to all parts of the area. Next, there must be a test of the voice with the music. Many times the music completely drowns out the words, and so the fashion message is lost. Acoustics are different when a hall is filled from when it is empty, so arrangements should be made to have several persons, stationed at various places in the room, who will give pre-arranged signals as to whether or not the commentator can be heard over the music. An electrician who understands the microphone should be on hand to deal with those microphone failures that seem to be an inevitable phenomenon of every public occasion.

There are times when the store will want to bring in an outside commentator. For the elaborate fashion revue, a screen, stage or radio star may be asked to be a master of ceremonies-commentator. Such people are great drawing cards, because of their fame and their showmanship. They may be difficult to handle, however, for they often know nothing about the fashion business. A script must be prepared for them. They must be briefed before the performance, if there is no time for a rehearsal. If it is at all possible, there should be a rehearsal. Even with a script and with briefing they sometimes make mistakes, but being show people, they will know how to turn a mistake into a laugh, and the audience will be delighted.

There are other special shows for which it is sometimes good to have an outside commentator, like the high school show or a show featuring a visiting designer or stylist. In all these cases, it is necessary to prepare some sort of script and to have at least one rehearsal. The commentator is a very important part of the show; he or she must perform well, or the show loses some of its value.

Chapter 12

How Do Fashion Shows Happen?

It is remarkable how much background knowledge is required, before we can come to the actual "blow-by-blow" account of how a fashion show is put together. What is the actual order of procedure and the best time schedule for doing a fashion show?

1. Possibly four weeks before the time scheduled for the fashion show, the fashion coordinator calls a meeting of the advertising manager, the display manager, the merchandise manager and any other executives who might be involved. At this meeting, the main objectives of the show will be determined — whether it is to be a prestige show, an educational show and so on; and toward what customers it is to be aimed. Some general ideas about the show will also be discussed. Methods of promoting the show will be discussed and at least partially decided. The approximate amount of money to be spent will be determined; and the time and place will be settled.

2. Following this policy decision meeting, the fashion coordinator goes to work immediately to translate her general idea for the show into a workable plan. She will work out a theme, assemble ideas for settings and action, make some plans about what should be shown, determine what props will be needed, list all the departments of the store which can be involved in the show and make notes of all matters which need further attention. She then calls a meeting of the ready-to-wear and accessory buyers and the buyers of other departments which may be part of the show. The display department should be represented, and the head carpenter, the electrician and the head of the porters should also be there.

But why do all these people have to be assembled to talk about a fashion show? It is because every one of them has some work to do for the show, and all should understand, *from the beginning*, what is going on. This single thing can save untold confusion, much individual explanation and running around. There is another reason, a psychological one even more powerful, why the fashion coordinator should call all these people together at the start of a fashion show. People who have to work on a project want and need to be consulted about it. They have good ideas to offer, and having become involved in the planning, they will spare nothing to see that the affair is a success.

One of the worst mistakes a fashion coordinator can make is to think that she knows all the answers to fashion show production. No single person is in possession of all knowledge, and no one person can ever carry through such a complicated matter single-handed. Sometimes, the fashion director of a store, knowing subconsciously that she doesn't know everything, and mistakenly believing that she must never let anyone discover this fact, does many things to upset others and to endanger the success of the show. The most intelligent, the safest and the best way to assure a good show is to ask help from those who know the various aspects of the situation thoroughly. Far from thinking that the fashion coordinator is shirking her duties, if she consults them, they will rally around to suggest good ideas and to do the work required.

One word of caution must, however, be added: *the fashion coordinator must never for one moment forget that she, and she alone, is responsible for the show.* Having consulted people, having benefited by their suggestions, having been assured of their cooperation, *she* must see that everything is carried through according to schedule. This means work — plenty of hard work. It does not mean sitting in an office and dictating memos to others, shifting the final responsibility upon their shoulders. If the fashion coordinator can think of herself as a theatrical producer — the woman who carries the full load of seeing that the "show goes on" — then at the end of her labors she will be assured of a good performance.

At the meeting of buyers and other key people, the plans for the show are outlined and discussed. Merchandise for the show will be considered, and the importance of having adequate stocks in all departments to take advantage of customers' requests will be emphasized. The date of the show may have to be shifted to insure having stocks on hand, for the show must sell goods and *goods must be on hand to be sold*. The settings will be considered, with the carpenter and display man advising as to the practicality of the coordinator's ideas. Certain assignments of tasks will be made immediately. Finally, dates for fittings and rehearsals will be determined. At this point, it may be decided to make the dress rehearsal a performance for the employees, in which case arrangements about this will have to be assigned.

During this all-important meeting, the fashion office secretary should take down the proceedings, so that immediately afterwards, a condensed memorandum can be sent to each person who attended. This memorandum will list under the name of each person, the things he or she has agreed to do and the time when a report should be made to the fashion coordinator. Any misunderstandings can be cleared up immediately, in this way, and the fashion office also has a record of what was decided and how it is to be accomplished.

3. From this point, the fashion coordinator becomes the production manager, and like all production managers, she should be the sole boss of the project. When the actual work of putting the show together starts, there can be only *one* head, one person who makes the final decisions, right or wrong. If this is not adhered to without deviation, the show will be a failure. Just as "too many cooks spoil the broth," too many bosses ruin a fashion show. This does not mean that the producer is not open to ideas and changes as the work progresses; it merely means that the producer accepts or rejects the ideas, makes the final decisions about what is and what is not to be done. The order of business from this point on is as follows:

a) The idea for the show must be put into logical, step-by-step form. Such questions as the following must be answered:

How many scenes in the show?

What will be their order?

What merchandise will be shown in each scene?

What sequence will be followed in showing these clothes?

What action can be used to give variety to the show?

When these questions have been answered, and the ideas have been written in proper order, a simplified playlet has really been written. Some of the script may be changed, but the skeleton plan has been set up.

b) The final plans for promoting the show must now be made. Invitations, if there are to be any, must be prepared; the program must be designed and put into production; ads must be scheduled and prepared; publicity photographs must be taken; releases written; press showings arranged and the press invited in plenty of time; radio interviews and spots must be arranged and written.

c) At the same time, the models for the show will be called in for fittings. For the average show, there should never be fewer than eight models and ten are preferable. It takes about one minute for a model to walk on the runway, one minute for her to get back to the dressing room and seven minutes for her to make a complete costume change. This time table is for experienced models; inexperienced models take longer, so more models will be needed. In general, it is never advisable to use more than twenty-five models for a show.

d) Arrangements must be made for dressers — one dresser to every two or three models, depending upon the intricacy of the costume changes and the experience of the models. Assistants in the fashion office, or competent people from the ready-to-wear departments — perhaps heads of stock or assistant buyers — should be assigned to the supervisory jobs back-stage. One dressing room supervisor checks the line-up and sees that models are ready as scheduled; one stage supervisor holds the script and stands at the stage entrance where the commentator can see her and sends the models out at the proper time.

e) Arrangements for changes of scenes must be made; or, if there are to be no changes but merely one background, this must be arranged for. In cases where there are scene changes, it is essential that as many persons as are needed to make the changes quickly be provided and that they be rehearsed thoroughly. Each one must be given specific duties to eliminate confusion and delays. One person is assigned to open and close the curtain, when the script demands it. This person may also be able to manage the lights; if not, another should be responsible.

f) The alteration room should be notified about the show and when the clothes will be ready for pressing and needed for the dress rehearsal and performance. Occasionally, clothes can be pressed after the dress rehearsal, but most often, there is not sufficient time between the two.

g) Musicians must be engaged, usually for the rehearsal and the performance. Sometimes, money can be saved merely by having the leader present for the rehearsal; it is then his responsibility to coach the other musicians regarding the musical requirements for the performance. Musicians should be union musicians; failure in this respect exposes the store to serious difficulties with labor groups in the community.

h) Fitting for a show during the day has one main advantage; it can be worked into the regular business day and, therefore, does not require special store arrangements. Its disadvantages are that fittings, even when there is a good-sized dressing room for the models, are disrupters on the floor, upsetting the salespeople and sometimes the customers. It is also difficult to accessorize costumes when they are fitted during the day.

Night fittings simplify the proceedings immeasurably, even though they necessitate keeping the floor open after hours. In preparation for night fittings, buyers of accessory departments are asked to send a representative of the department (probably the assistant buyer) to the fittings with a good selection of her stock in accordance with suggestions submitted in advance by the fashion coordinator. Tables should be set up, upon which these accessories will be arranged. As each model is fitted with her dress or suit, she goes to the accessory tables, where the fashion coordinator selects the bag, gloves, jewelry, scarfs to be used. The model then goes to the millinery department and selects one or two hats for the fashion coordinator's final approval; she gets the shoes which have been suggested as suitable for this costume. She also has a fitter from the alteration department check the evenness of her hem and make any minor, necessary adjustments. When all the accessories have been chosen, the fashion assistant lists them, with the dress, on the model's sheet of paper on which are recorded all this individual's costumes for the show. The departmental assistants also record on their transfer of merchandise books the items to be used in the show. In this way, both the fashion department and the merchandise department have accurate checks on the goods in the show. These records are also the source of information necessary for making up the program copy and for listing the line-up for the show. Prices of all items should be listed on both records.

Since fittings can be done at night in much less time than during the day, this method is especially good when the store does not wish to keep its goods out of stock any longer than is absolutely necessary. Provided everything has been worked out very completely in advance, a show can be fitted, rehearsed and presented in three days.

When it is necessary to have fittings during the day, the models get the clothes, hats and shoes they are to show, and the fashion assistant makes a list of accessories required for each outfit. Later, the assistant gathers these accessories from the various departments and has them ready, when the models come for the dress rehearsal.

i) As soon as all the clothes have been selected and recorded on the model's fitting sheets, the fashion coordinator can plan the line-up for the show. This line-up (the order in which models will appear on the runway) is determined by the action of the show and the order in which the coordinator wishes to show the clothes. It is also planned, so that each model will be allowed sufficient time for her changes of costume. When very experienced models are used, each one can appear every ninth time in the show; thus it is necessary to have only eight models.

The line-up provides the copy for the program, for the clothes must be listed in the program in the order in which they are shown on the runway. Having made accurate notes about each outfit to be shown, the coordinator can merely refer to the line-up and the model's fitting sheet to get all the necessary information for the program. Of course, if the show is to be done in scenes, then appropriate headings must be written to carry out the theme of the show.

One most important question is to be answered, when the program copy is prepared: "Shall we give the prices of the garments on the program?" The answer, for most merchandisers, is an emphatic "Yes!" Customers *want* to know how much the clothes they are seeing cost. If the audience is responsive, every person in it will be thinking in terms of buying some of the merchandise shown. Therefore, every one will want to know the cost involved. Since fashion shows are given for the purpose of selling goods, everything must be done to encourage those sales, and giving prices is a sure way of accomplishing this main purpose.

Since the program cover has already been designed and printed, all that is needed is the inside copy, and it is rushed to the printer as quickly as possible. Whenever possible, two days should be allowed, but sometimes the job can be rushed through in a day and a half. It is never safe to work so close, except when it is absolutely impossible to do otherwise. The earlier the copy is received by the printer, the better the chances for a good job.

j) The number of rehearsals necessary for a show depends upon the elaborateness of the show and the competence of the performers. Rehearsals should be kept at a minimum, both because they are expensive and because they take much time. Here, again, good advance planning can simplify matters greatly. Often, it is

MODEL'S FITTING SHEET

Name.. Date of Show............................

Scene (If Any)	Garment–Price	Hat–Price	Handbag–Price	Gloves–Price	Shoes–Price	Miscellaneous (Luggage, sports equipment, props)

a good idea to have a business rehearsal before the fittings. At this rehearsal, the models are given an outline of the show and are rehearsed in their parts. This is especially advisable when the show is a dramatized one, for the models must know what pantomime they are to do. This business rehearsal can be held just before the fittings, if it is difficult to get everyone together too often.

The dress rehearsal should be given, whenever possible, the evening before the performance with all the store employees as guests or, if all employees cannot be accommodated, for those in the fashion departments. Having this audience for the dress rehearsal has many advantages. First, performers always respond to an audience, and thus the fashion coordinator can see how the show will actually appear at the regular performance. Also, all employees who need this knowledge can learn the fashion story from seeing the rehearsal; and last, employees are customers of the store, and may be inspired to purchases by the show.

Every phase of the show should be rehearsed at the dress rehearsal: settings should be ready and changed, if this is to be done; lights should be used; music should be used as required; the commentary should be given; the costumes should be complete; back-stage people should do their parts; line-ups should be posted in the dressing room. This is also the time when the fashion coordinator can make notes on any changes which should be made. Perhaps, she will decide that a certain costume is not perfectly accessorized. She notes this fact on the card for that outfit; later, having asked the model to wait after the rehearsal, she makes the change.

After the dress rehearsal, each model, with the help of her dresser, sees that all her accessories are in her accessory boxes, stacked on her section of the dressing table. The dressers also see that the clothes of the models they assist are in the correct order for the performance, as listed on the line-up posted on the dressing room wall.

k) The fashion show must start promptly at the time stated, and it should never last longer than one hour. It is often better to have it last fifty minutes. This means that the maximum number of costumes to be shown is fifty. Longer shows and more merchandise have proved exhausting to audiences. It is always better to send an audience away wishing that there had been more show, than to have them worn out and disgusted because the show was so long. Wishing for more puts them into a mood to buy; being tired and disgusted makes them want to go home instead.

A number of things must be checked before the show is ready to start. This checking can be done by the fashion assistant, if there is one, but *it must be done* by someone who is thoroughly trustworthy. The following are to be checked:

(1) That ushers know what time doors are to be opened.
(2) That programs are ready for distribution.
(3) That any favors to be distributed are ready.
(4) That all changes decided upon at the dress rehearsal have been made.
(5) That all clothes are on the racks in the proper order.
(6) That all accessories are in the boxes of each model. (Large hat boxes can be used for bags, gloves, jewelry, etc.)
(7) That the microphone is in order.
(8) That stage settings are in order.
(9) That all props are available.
(10) That the lights are in order.

l) When the final curtain has been pulled, there is a tendency, which is only natural, to heave a great sigh and relax. This, alas, is precisely what the fashion department does not dare to do at this point. A well-trained staff — models, dressers, assistants — know what they are supposed to do immediately after the show; this knowledge can prevent much confusion and sometimes even loss of merchandise.

Every piece which has been presented in the show must get back to its department as quickly as possible, because customers may want to buy the very things they saw in the show. Therefore, the dressers must see that all garments, properly fastened and zippered, are hung on the racks according to the departments from which they came. For instance, all goods from Department

19, suits, should be together; all coats from a certain department should be together, etc. The models should do the same thing with the accessories. One should gather all the hats, another the gloves, still another the handbags, etc.

The departments, in the meantime, should have sent the head of stock or assistant to the dressing room with the lists of goods taken from each department. The goods are then checked against the records and a copy, signed by the department representative and the fashion department representative, perhaps the model, is given to the fashion coordinator. This is her record that all stock has been received by the various departments in good condition. This procedure can save many bad experiences for the fashion department. When everything has been checked, it can be removed immediately to the selling floor. If this is properly systemized, all goods can thus be returned within a half hour after the show, and sometimes less.

m) As soon after the show as possible — probably the next morning — the fashion coordinator writes a report about the show to be sent to the various store executives — merchandise manager, advertising manager, owner, etc. — who are concerned with the promotion. This report should be brief but comprehensive and should include the following:

(1) Departments of the store represented in the show.

(2) Merchandise shown and kind of show presented.

(3) Number of people who attended the show. If dress rehearsal was for employees, this fact should be noted.

(4) Direct sales resulting from show. This is a difficult figure to arrive at, but buyers might reasonably include sales immediately after the show, telephone orders the next day, and any other sales the next day which can be traced directly to the show.

(5) Total expense of the show.

(6) Kinds of publicity obtained for the show, including radio interviews and free newspaper lineage.

A carbon copy of this report should, of course, be kept in the fashion office files. With it, another report or series of notes, which the fashion coordinator makes for her own information, should be filed. These notes will include ideas for improving subsequent shows in any particular. For instance, certain procedures may have been used for a certain show that could well be used again in a similar show. Also information about models and their particular abilities could be noted here and on the model's card as well. These notes are invaluable in improving the techniques of show production.